The Gliders

Alan Lloyd's established international reputation covers a wide field of history, biography and fiction. Several of his books have been military histories, and military interest is reflected in others. His non-fiction has received consistent critical acclaim for readability, balanced judgement and factual accuracy, and has been listed among the outstanding books of its year by *The Times*, praised by academic authorities as well as the popular press, and acclaimed by such distinguished writers and historians as Mary Renault and A.J.P. Taylor.

The Gliders

ALAN LLOYD

ARROW BOOKS

Arrow Books Limited
62–65 Chandos Place, London WC2N 4NW

An imprint of Century Hutchinson Limited

London Melbourne Sydney Auckland
Johannesburg and agencies throughout
the world

First published in Great Britain by Leo Cooper in
association with Martin Secker & Warburg Ltd 1982
Arrow edition 1989

© Alan Lloyd 1982

Printed and bound in Great Britain by
The Guernsey Press Co. Ltd, Guernsey, Channel Islands.

ISBN 0 09 957460 8

Contents

Author's Note

Today they are busy in different jobs—an advertising manager, a civil servant, newsagents, a confectionery salesman, a technical representative. Once, they were volunteers in one of the most hazardous and exceptional of military services. This is primarily, though not exclusively, their story: an account of the British glider men. The names of most who helped in its preparation, whether by lending log-books, manuscripts and other documents, or by granting interviews, are in the text. To all of them—the many who welcomed me at their homes, and those who travelled to the old farmhouse through the summer—I am indebted and express my thanks. I am also most grateful for the information provided by Captain J. R. Cross, Librarian of the Museum of Army Flying, Middle Wallop, and to Mr A. J. Hollingdale, General Secretary of the Glider Pilot Regimental Association, for his assistance.

Alan Lloyd
Kent 1982

Prelude: Brood of the Wasserkuppe

In November 1940, as the last leaves of a fateful summer tumbled like fallen nations at Hitler's feet, the Führer and his deputy, Rudolph Hess, discussed the final bastion opposing them, the British Isles. The key to England, Hess thought, might be an extraordinary weapon he had heard about. It was, quite simply, a monstrous glider, a kind of flying barracks capable of lifting 200 fully-equipped storm troops, or the equivalent weight in tanks and guns.

The idea of using gliders to carry troops was not new. Germany had already employed them in the conquest of Europe, but her standard assault glider lifted a mere section of infantry, its operations so far successful but small scale. The notion that a glider might transport an entire company of soldiers, even tanks, seemed incredible.

It had been put to Hess by Willy Messerschmitt. At forty-two, Professor Messerschmitt, tall and stubborn-jawed, the son of a Frankfurt wine merchant, had climbed to prominence in the aircraft industry from small beginnings in the glider field. In 1916, he had precociously constructed and flown a sailplane which had remained airborne for the then considerable time of two and a half minutes. After the First World War he had been well known among the gliding enthusiasts of the centres which flourished in the Harz and Rhon mountains, notably the famed gliding eyries of the Wasserkuppe.

Now, with France occupied and the British at bay in their island fastness, Messerschmitt was convinced that the monster glider he proposed to Hess was practical. In this he had the assurances of the experienced head of design at his company, Woldemar Voigt, and the chief of construction, Joseph Froelich. It remained to get the Führer's permission to go ahead.

Already, Hitler had decided that mass glider landings would spearhead his invasion of southern England, the operation code-named *Seelöwe*, or Sea Lion. Five hundred gliders of the standard type were to be released from tow-planes high over the coast of France and swoop silently to the flats and downs of Kent and East Sussex to secure the first footing on British soil. A prime advantage of gliders, claimed their advocates, was that their mainly wooden structure made accurate radar detection difficult. There would be little warning in England of their approach.

But there was a drawback crucial to the mass use of airborne forces: no aircraft yet known, powered or otherwise, came near to lifting a tank or a heavy gun, and without such supports the assault units would not be able to resist armoured counter-attack. In this light, the giant glider project had huge appeal, both as a means of landing armour by air and for the unique troop capacity of each plane.

Almost immediately, Hitler expressed approval and work on the so-designated Me321, the *Gigant* or Giant, was put in hand. Nothing like it had been seen on an airfield. It had a veritable barn of a fuselage and its wing-span, 181 ft, was not merely unique at that period but destined to remain so for three decades—until the Boeing 747 flew. Within four months of work commencing, the Giant was test-flown.

Early trials showed that it handled well once aloft, but getting it there, especially when loaded, was hazardous. Indeed, no single aircraft possessed by the Germans proved sufficiently powerful to tow the monster and its cargo into the air, and various multiples of tow-planes were hitched to it. At one stage, three twin-engined Me 110s were used like sled horses in *troika* harness. Between them they generated enough power, but losses due to the perils of the operation were so costly the technique was given up.

The final resort was as extraordinary as the Giant itself.

It was suggested by General Ernst Udet, flamboyant air ace of the first war, whose stocky figure had been among those familiar on the Wasserkuppe. Two Heinkel He 111 bombers were joined at the wings to form a single plane, the four engines thus provided supplemented by a fifth where their wings met. It did the trick. Aided by booster rockets clamped to the glider, the flying Siamese twin hauled the Giant aloft. Wasteful of machines, it was not wholly to the liking of the Luftwaffe, but objections were overruled and the first Giants hurried to France for the ultimate stride to the Führer's goal.

German interest in gliders had trenchant roots. When Field Marshal Hindenburg had acknowledged defeat in 1918, hundreds of young German fliers, accustomed to the thrill of the skies, found themselves wingless and unemployed in a broken nation. The only cheap way to fly again was to emulate the great German pioneer Otto Lilienthal and sail glide-planes. At Lilienthal's death in a flying accident, the words of Leonardo da Vinci had been inscribed on his monument:

> The great artificial bird will some day set out upon its first flight from a hilltop. It will fill the universe with wonder and all books with its fame. And the nest where the bird was born shall be glorious . . .

For the unwanted, largely impoverished, fighter and bomber pilots of defeated Germany, the symbolic nest was the Wasserkuppe, a towering height above the small town of Gersfeld, to which they dragged their sketchy sailplanes at weekends to snatch a few precious minutes above the slopes. For most, it was the sheer need to fly which prompted gliding—'A yearning for something higher, in the best sense,' explained ex-Gotha pilot Hermann Steiner, 'when life seemed all but hopeless and without point.'

But for some, the craze had a fiercer edge. Twenty-two years almost to the day before Hitler and Hess discussed the Giant, a group of First World War fighter pilots gathered in a beer cellar at Aschaffenberg, Bavaria, for a farewell spree before departing to civilian life. Outside, a hostile crowd sporting the red arm-bands of the revolutionary councils jeered noisily. At last, a thin-lipped officer spoke angrily. Hermann Goering, successor in command to the legendary Manfred Richthofen, was noted for his military zeal and rigid discipline. Now, in a diatribe against the traitors and faint-hearts of the nation, the future chief of the Luftwaffe was adamant. The air force had not been beaten. 'The new fight has started,' he rasped; 'our day will come again.'

Four years later, Goering confided the importance of German gliding to a former adversary, American ace Eddie Rickenbacker. The Treaty of Versailles had strictly limited powered flying in Germany but, said Goering, 'it is by air power that we shall regain the German empire. First, we must teach gliding as a sport to the youth of Germany.'

To Hermann Goering and his associates, gliding presented the perfect discipline within which to cultivate the air-consciousness of young Germans, to instil the knowledge of aerodynamics and basic aviation which would give the air force of the future quite literally a flying start. It was also, as a cover for that ambition, immaculate. Few sports were more pacific than planing serenely as a sailing bird. It was the antithesis of violence.

And so, through the political confusion of the twenties, a growing band of youthful pilgrims paid homage at the Wasserkuppe to the aces of powerless flight, men such as Robert Kronfeld the 'storm rider' (himself a Jew and anti-Nazi), Ferdinand Schulz of the 'flying broomstick', Wolf

Hirth, Max Kegel, Edgar Dittmar, many more. By 1930, the world of competitive glider flying was dominated by German pilots.

Amidst the purists appeared increasingly those whose aims went beyond sport. Early among them was a handsome war veteran, Kurt Student, and his lovely wife. The couple took a solicitous interest in the often impecunious enthusiasts. Soon Captain Student was arranging funds for them. That such welcome help came from the military budget was not mentioned, but hints were dropped that a semi-martial approach to future glider trials might be circumspect.

Student, later to command Hitler's crack 7th Airborne Division, was already an agent of the Truppenamt, cloaked version of an outlawed general staff now dedicated to the revival of German armed might.

Gradually, as Hitler's star rose, the harnessing of glider sport to the rebirth of the *Reichswehr* became overt. By the thirties, a slim stone column had been raised on the Wasserkuppe to the power of flight. 'Fly, Germans,' exhorted the words at its base, 'and you will conquer.' Through the youth movement of the National Socialist party, all young Germans were urged to take up gliding. Members of the Hitler Youth could start training at the age of 14 and received an advanced certificate after logging two hours of flying time. Another certificate, issued after 20 hours, became a required qualification for Luftwaffe candidates.

It was thorough. Logs were kept meticulously, records passed to the air ministry. Instruction was given in navigation, wireless and other skills. And it spawned, as planned, a huge reservoir of potential combat crews.

Nor were the glider eyries mere nurseries for personnel. Through the early thirties it began to dawn on German military circles that the glider itself—the gentle dove exploited to outwit Versailles—might be bred to perform hawkish feats. Among others, the punchy and imaginative General Ernst Udet championed the notion that gliders, towed by warplanes, could be used to land and supply troops.

As war came near, the standard German troop glider, a high-winged ship with a 72-ft span and a cargo lift of 2,800 lbs (9 equipped troops), emerged as a refinement of a civil prototype first tested by a woman gliding enthusiast, Hanna Reitsch. As slight as she was fearless, Reitsch later joined the succession of test pilots who struggled to get Messerschmitt's Giant aloft. The smaller plane, known as the DFS 230, was less troublesome.

In 1939, Kurt Student flew and admired the craft. No longer 'under-cover', Student, now a colonel, took command of its military development. He had no doubt about its coming role. While others saw it primarily as a transport adjunct, Student christened the DFS 230 an 'attack glider'. The next few months were to prove just how right he was.

At the glimmer of dawn, 10 May, 1940, a formation of venerable three-engined Ju 52s lumbered from Cologne towards Liège and Belgium's 'impregnable' Fort Eben Emael. Behind each of ten planes, attached by tow-line, rode a laden DFS 230 in sombre warpaint.

The Belgian stronghold had been built five years earlier to withstand air bombardment or ground attack. An awesome obstacle to Hitler's *Blitzkrieg*, its steel and concrete casemates protected a teeming garrison beneath almost half a mile of armoured turrets and bristling cupolas. Its capture, German generals had advised, would involve a slogging battle and heavy losses, perhaps five or six thousand men. Hitler had neither time nor the troops to spare. He called for an audacious stroke.

A mile from the objective, a few minutes after five o'clock, the gliders cut loose from their tugs and swooped quietly, wind whistling in wing-braces, on the great fort. Flying them were glider pilots who had learned their skills with the clubs of the Rhon and on the Wasserkuppe.

The descent was consummate. One by one the ships flopped to the roof of the stronghold, slewed to a standstill and burst open. Through doors and fabric of fuselage erupted sappers with explosives and Schmeisser pistols. Within 30 minutes, the turrets of Eben Emael had been devastated, observation posts blown assunder, exits blocked. So complete was surprise that 70-odd glider troops, led by a lieutenant, Rudolf Witzig, were able to hold the roof until the fort surrendered next morning. The cost to them in dead was less than a dozen men.

At the same time, more gliders slid through the rising mists of the Meuse river to pitch stealthily near bridges vital to the thrust of Hitler's armoured groups. Two were seized intact from their defenders, despite the fact that demolition charges were in place on them. The extraordinary advent of the gliders completely confused the guards.

Eben Emael, proof of the 'irresistibility' of the *Wehrmacht* as propaganda chief Joseph Goebbels proclaimed the feat, was world news. Much was made of the capture, but German reports omitted the glider role. Attack gliders, the Führer had decided, were 'top security'. He had plans to spring the surprise again.

A handful of gliders had dived on Belgium; hundreds, as the overture to *Seelöwe*, would land in England. Production of DFS 230s, supervised by the Gotha company, was speeded, the craft shuttled west as France crumpled. Student surveyed his sky troops restlessly. Allowed to unleash them promptly, he believed he could deal London a knockout blow. But Teutonic thoroughness prevailed over impulse. As Dunkirk passed, the Führer waited, resolved to launch *Seelöwe* with every care. Among other things, he wanted the new Giants to be at readiness.

Part One

Norway to Normandy

I

An Uncertain Flame

British gliding, thriving on a club basis before the war, was the sport of individualists for whom the Nazi concept of regimented recreation was anathema. Not only were war gliders alien to their spirit, the war itself was a nuisance they forgot in their little sailplanes. Despite a ban on private flying, weekend enthusiasts, with or without the connivance of Air Force stations, were still aloft the English downlands as France fell. On Dunstable Downs, near Luton, sporting gliders blithely sailed until Whitsun 1940, despite the bombs of the Luftwaffe and straffing Messerschmitts.

Not until Dunkirk was it whispered among members at the club bars that gliding might have more than, say, golf or cricket to contribute to the fighting war.

It had been in Churchill's mind since Eben Emael. Unlike the general public, the prime minister was aware of the role played in the downfall of Europe by air troops. That Britain had none—among the lesser worries of her shaken staff as they braced for *Seelöwe*—vexed the premier. In a terse note to his commanders he demanded an airborne force.

The proposal, that darkest eve in England since Napoleon, verged on impudence. The force, to be prepared within ten months, was to be 5,000 strong, equipped with gliders and parachutes. Protests that defensive needs were too great to indulge the novelty received Churchillian scorn. A groping start was made.

At Dunstable, club members encountered the first sign that things were stirring when an ancient Kestrel glider was dusted of its cobwebs, packed in a trailer and consigned to a mysterious destination in the northwest. Soon afterwards, Lawrence Wright, an architect and experienced sporting pilot, then in his thirties, got a cryptic message from the club's gliding instructor to 'stand by'.

Tim Hervey, the instructor, a flying veteran of the first war and one-time stunt pilot, was a respected elder of the gliding world. Like the Kestrel, he had vanished from Dunstable to an airfield near Manchester, Ringway, and something known as the Central Landing Establishment. So obscure was this entity that the War Office itself had misdirected correspondence to the Central Laundering Establishment.

Here, as a result of Churchill's initiative, a studious army major, John Rock of the engineers, had arrived to organise the new force. How, or in what constitution, was not explained. 'It was impossible,' he bemoaned, 'to obtain information as to policy.' But since he started, as a wit put it drily, from 'Rock bottom', basic equipment was the first need. Design clues were minimal: a captured German army parachute, intelligence files on Hitler's air brigades.

Rock squinted at them down a sharp nose. If the Central Landing Establishment were as vague in its objectives as in its title, its mixed bag of soldiers and airmen were enthusiasts. Wright, sent to Ringway to become chief ground instructor, found Hervey back in uniform in charge of glider training, and Robert Kronfeld, the Jewish ace who had escaped the Nazis, working on towing problems. Their task was daunting. Against Hitler's glider-readiness, Ringway was a nursery.

Its small fleet of gliders, like the mercy craft of Dunkirk, was a miscellaneous subscription from private ownership: Vikings, Kites, the Kestrel, a Condor, new and obsolete equally incongruous in battle-paint. Most were single-seaters designed for soaring. A prized two-seater survived a short time then shed its ailerons. In the context of war, the tugs, too, were risible. Some were Tiger Moths, others outdated biplane fighters of the Hart type. One, an Avro 504N, had towed advertising banners in better times, a model basically unaltered since 1913.

Elementary knowledge, possessed years since by the Germans, was gained the hard way. In the absence of military gliders, towing trials were carried out by hauling warplanes, Battles and Wellesleys, with their engines stopped. In some cases, propellers were removed from them. The best lengths for towropes were not known. Tests with excessive lengths found the sag still on the ground, inviting disaster, as the planes climbed. Too little rope, and the glider became airborne in the backspit of stationary tug when its engines revved.

Ambitiously, an earnest Kronfeld experimented with towing-lights for night hauls. But the enthusiasm of Rock and his colleagues was not ubiquitous. The War Office was far from agreed it needed glider troops. Those who favoured them faced the urgent priorities of defence, against which a doubtful future cast puny weight. It was a notable irony that when the unit moved home at the end of 1940 to Haddenham, Oxfordshire, its new field was strewn with old cars to obstruct German gliders; the personnel of a project based on offensive planning, armed with sharpened broomsticks for their defence.

By the new year, specifications for war gliders were complete and on the drawingboard. It had been fast work but, until the gliders could be made, little showed for it. Already, Churchill was restless about the glider scheme. 'Is it being seriously taken up?' he had asked the chief of staff in the autumn. April, the deadline, disappointed him.

Rock, too serious a man to relish showmanship, was faced with a prime minister anxious for a display. Six gliders were shown in flight. Of these, five were prewar sporting

sailplanes in war colours; one, an experimental prototype. It
was the best that was available. Scarcely more spectacular
were the paratroops. Five ponderous Whitley bombers took
off with 40 men, of whom six failed to emerge at the
dropping point. But at least Churchill admired the dagger
designed for them, flourishing it with a grim snarl.

'A sad story,' he huffed afterwards.

That 1942 would see the prime minister actually obliged to
curtail glider production due to excessive stock—he did not
want, he wrote, 'a lot of these things standing out in the rain
and spoiling'—was a succinct vindication of the early work.
Swift manufacture owed much to the Central Landing
Establishment. Rock's men had decided quickly what was
needed and were proved right. Modifications at trial stages
were few, mainly concerned with towing gear, and promptly
resolved by the pioneers.

Thereafter, wooden construction and the absence of
engines meant that gliders could be produced quicker, with
less strain on resources, than powered warplanes. Coach
builders and furniture-makers could be involved in manufacture. The Germans had employed a toy-making firm in their
own programme. General Aircraft, the company to produce
Britain's first military glider, the Hotspur, delivered the
prototype within four months of a production order. A
streamlined 8-seater of sporting pedigree, it was used very
largely as a training craft.

The standard British attack glider, designed by Airspeed
Aviation and built by Harris Lebus in southern England, was
named the Horsa. Bigger and less elegant than the Hotspur
or its enemy counterpart, the Horsa carried 25 troops and
could hold a jeep. It had a snub, bug-like nose, a high wing
almost halfway back on the fuselage and was about the size of
a Wellington bomber—67 ft in length, wing-span 80 ft. Fully
loaded it weighed rather more than 7 tons, half of which was
its own weight.

Horsa production followed that of the Hotspur by a few

months. Meanwhile, peacetime glider pilots were being transferred from other services. Assembled at Haddenham, they formed the instruction staff for the army pupils who soon arrived.

The initial intake, three officers, two sergeants and seven corporals, all volunteers, reported early in 1941. Some were experienced pilots of powered aircraft. The first to glide solo, a sergeant, had flown Messerschmitts in the Spanish Civil War. A week after his *début*, a corporal established another 'first' by landing on the roof of the sergeants' mess. Lawrence Wright, now preparing a glider training manual, recalled the period with insouciance, the carefree atmosphere. No one had thought of giving the pupils a medical, none had seen a combat glider, flying pay promised beforehand had not materialised. But it was spring, and army gliding seemed good sport.

Then, abruptly, German gliders stole the scene again. They flew not for England but the isle of Crete. On 20 May, the battle for Britain's Mediterranean base erupted with the first mass glider assault in fighting history. Its fate made for sombre contemplation at Haddenham.

At three minutes past five on a Tuesday morning, the first DFS 230 took the air from Eleusis, near captured Athens, and was joined by more than 70 others shortly afterwards. It might well have been from a field in France, but the Luftwaffe had failed to seize the day skies of England whereas Crete lay shorn of air defence. The day before, the last of its handful of warplanes, most obsolete, had withdrawn to Egypt in the face of 1,280 German machines opposed to them. There remained AA guns, but these would be neutralised by bomber raids.

Already, Hitler's plans of conquest had turned to Russia, but first Crete would secure his lanes to Rommel and North Africa.

The attack by air armada, the flame of the Hitler Youth, would be Goering's prodigious triumph and sweet revenge.

Its code name *Merkur*—Mercury the winged god—was sufficiently unsubtle to make the point. General Student was put in charge. Among his forces were those which mounted the Eben Emael strike.

Tight security had covered the movement of men and gliders by train from Germany through Bulgaria towards the airfields in occupied Greece where they would take off. Among precautions, all clues to the airborne nature of the troops had been removed from uniforms and documents, but Britain's agents in Greece were watchful, the German staffs in Athens less than circumspect. Unknown to Student, London had never been so well informed of a German move.

'It seems clear,' Churchill had telegraphed Middle East headquarters before the gliders left Hildesheim, Germany, 'that a heavy airborne attack by German troops and bombers will be made on Crete.'

In fact, Crete had itself been warned ten days earlier. But the island was far removed from help and under German air control. General Sir Bernard Freyberg, commanding, had few illusions. He felt, however, he could beat off an air invasion provided it was not joined by sea assault. To this extent he was as deceived as were Student's glider pilots, who believed they had come to Greece in the greatest secrecy.

Student chatted to them on the airfields. He was still a handsome man with a knack of putting men at ease, and shook hands with the pilots and wished them luck. They were confident. Nothing in their experience, from Belgium to a series of minor glider attacks in the Greek campaign, undermined hopes. The weather was clear; the Luftwaffe ruled the Balkan and Aegean skies.

That was vital. Gliders under tow were defenceless targets for hostile warplanes, and the flight south over 200 miles of water was perilous. The absence of British aircraft was good news.

Steadily, gliders and tugs cleared the Greek coast and made for Crete, their main objective Maleme airport in the northwest. Ahead, bombers of the German 8th Air Corps attacked the island's anti-aircraft batteries. Behind, 400 transport aeroplanes followed with paratroops. White-frilled islands slid below in a sparkling sea.

Aboard one glider was the commander of the 7th Air Division, Lieutenant-General Wilhelm Seussman. According to ground staff, Seussman and his aides had packed too much equipment in the aircraft, which adopted from the outset a strange attitude. Soon, it was struggling on its towline like a hooked fish. Twenty minutes from Eleusis, above Aegina, it disintegrated, plunging its occupants to death on the isle below. Its wings had exploded, internal pressures triggered by erratic flight.

Ploughing past the airborne debris, the rest flew on while Seussman's tug turned back, towline dangling. Heinkels and Stukas were still hammering Crete as the twin promontories of the Bay of Canea came in view. The fleet had been airborne for two hours. Five gliders were in the water; 66 prepared to cut free. Silently the swarm descended to the scrubby coast.

They came in low from the sea in a grey mass. On the ground, a correspondant for *The Times* watched them as, 'ominous in the sky', they drew near. 'I saw the first four, big ones of 70-feet wingspread, come over Suda Bay promontory. It seemed as if they were diving straight on top of me. But in the last minute they banked and wheeled.' Around Maleme, the defenders gawped as the fleet approached. Scarcely a gun fired; the island's six Hurricanes had flown out.

The airport and surrounding country was held by New Zealanders. They had taken a pounding from the Luftwaffe and their mood was grim. Bracing, they lashed the gliders with every rifle and machine-gun which came to bear. Inexorably, the first four ships flew on beyond a low hill. There, moments, later, *The Times* reporter found them frozen in tableaux of macabre calm. Not a single man was alive in them.

Murderous ground fire drilled other craft, whipping through canvas and wooden spars. Some, now flown by dead men, hit hillsides, compacting like concertinas, or cartwheeled from trees strewing passengers. Some broke up as they crashed; some in the air, chopped by vicious fire. One struck an outcrop of Crete's metamorphic rock. Another, in headlong flight, rammed an iron bridge. Often, they came down near well-camouflaged defence posts. 'Many,' said a witness, 'delivered their cargoes to sudden death. Stunned and bewildered air troops reeled out into a hail of bullets from close range.'

Crippled gliders clawed above torn wrecks. It was a tribute to the skill and bravery of the pilots that few came down far from their targets, however haplessly.

While the lucky ones contributed at least small parties to the week-long struggle which ended in German conquest, losses—'exceptionally high and bloody' in the words of the German battle summary—were truly terrible. Shocked despite victory, Student later concurred with Churchill that Crete was the graveyard of his air troops, the only such force Hitler then possessed. 'Gliders,' concluded a British witness, 'were a failure', and German policy henceforth sustained the view. Nazi leaders lost interest in their combat role.

Indeed, after Crete the Germans switched their gliders almost wholly to freighter tasks, especially ferrying supplies to the Russian front. From its early glory in Belgium, the DFS 230 was retired to so-called Cargo Glider Towing Groups together with the unblooded Giant from Messerschmitt. Two hundred Giants rolled from the factory, but they continued to present towing problems and many were converted as powered aircraft.

It was a strange trick of timing that Germany, the one nation experienced in the use of combat gliders, should abandon them just as Britain entered the fighting glider field. At Haddenham the Crete reports were not bright reading. 'Depressing data for our future use; we did not emphasise the details,' an instructor wrote.

2

Freshmen

Three years after Student had first flown the DFS 230, British pilots were getting to know the Horsa glider. It was a new thrill. The cockpit was a veritable greenhouse in which two fliers sat side-by-side with a fine view. Each had a spade-grip control column and rudder bars. An elementary flying panel contained three instruments: an airspeed indicator, an altimeter and a 'blind flying' device, the so-called 'angle of dangle', which denoted the glider's tow position.

Beside the pilots were two handles, one for the huge flaps which could be set at 45 or 90 degrees when required, and one for releasing the towline. The line, attached by a Y-junction to two points on the wings, contained the telephone cable to the tow-plane. For take-off, the tug slowly took up the slack, the wheel-brakes of the glider were released and the combination gained speed. At about 70 mph, the glider lifted off before the tug was airborne.

The position was now 'high-tow'. In level flight, the pilot might drop his glider through the slipstream of the tug to fly slightly below it, at 'low-tow', where the line was more clearly visible. Like all gliders, the Horsa was a handful in towed flight, but once released became, as a pilot put it, 'incredibly smooth, a strange silence in the cockpit'.

In tow, speeds of up to 160 mph were safe, if improbable. In free flight the glide was about 80 mph loaded, losing roughly 1,000 ft for every 2,500 yds flown. The ship was superbly tolerant. Stalling was no worry, and with flaps down a pilot could descend with a fantastically steep 1 in 1$\frac{1}{2}$ flight path, levelling off to land just above stalling incidence.

Like bees in spring, these novel aircraft appeared increasingly over the scarred and ancient chalk downs of southern England as Britain's first airborne army, a division under the slight and dapper Major-General 'Boy' Browning, began to take shape in 1942.

At the centre of activity was an undulating and rabbit-bitten airfield, Netheravon on Salisbury Plain, revered for a flying history which predated 1913, when Bristol Box Kites had risen there. Now its squadrons were under Group Captain Sir Nigel Norman, an early and effervescent war glider enthusiast. Not far off, at Tilshead, the bleak huts of an old artillery range served as a depot for what, under Rock, had become the Glider Pilot Regiment.

As his second, Rock was assigned a forceful major named George Chatterton, swiftly to make his solid presence felt.

Until now, the glider unit had assumed a predominantly RAF character. Technologically and air orientated, its personnel had been bound by bonds of craftsmanship and common interest rather than drilled disciplines. Rock himself, though a soldier, was not a drill-square officer. A product of staff college, he spoke four languages, was quiet in manner, intellectual in approach to the job at hand.

By contrast, Chatterton, in gleaming top boots and Sam Browne, was galvanising. Arriving when Rock was on a flying course, he had soon introduced Guards sergeant-majors to the depot, put up posters on deportment and invoked the spirit of Cromwell in a brisk address. He would, he announced, be 'quite ruthless', tolerating 'only the best' in discipline. Those who did not like it should get out.

Suddenly, men were marching to meals and lectures, even to gliders. It brought some smirks from the RAF and complaints from others whose preconceptions of the new force were upset. Not least among them was Rock, who told his second-in-command to ease off. 'I could see,' wrote Chatterton, 'he did not approve of my spit and polish methods . . . I argued with him.' To Rock's supporters, Chatterton was a disruptive anachronism; to Chatterton's supporters, a more soldierly emphasis in glider pilot training was overdue.

One night Rock took off on a trial flight in a glider laden with sandbags to simulate a combat cargo. As the combination rose, the towline snapped and, attempting an emergency landing, Rock struck a pole in the darkness, a ton of sandbags crushing the cockpit bulwark. Rock's death marked a watershed for Britain's glider force. The pioneer was gone; the new leader took over. The first parade attended by a fresh intake of pupils was Rock's funeral. 'It was a bit unnerving,' recalls one of the trainees, John Griffiths. 'I wondered what I was in for. Major Chatterton enlightened us.'

The man who was to build the regiment was a complex character. 'He was a brilliant pilot,' recalls a fellow officer, 'and a great talker. He could stand up in front of men and enthrall them with words. He gave the force a soul and personality.' Behind the polish and insistence on discipline lay an engaging impishness. Chatterton, his comrades learned, was a scintillating party-turn. Lawrence Wright discerned in him a born actor, and indeed his life had spanned many parts.

A naval cadet at Pangbourne, he had later joined the RAF, flown with a celebrated aerobatic team, retired with crash injuries and served in France with the army before Dunkirk. Both experience and nature defied labelling.

Arriving at Tilshead less confident than he looked, Chatterton had surveyed a chill winter scene and pondered 'deep and long' the requirements of a combat glider pilot. Flying a loaded craft on tow, the lives of its occupants in his hands, would impose a severe strain. On landing, thought Chatterton, an Air Force pilot desired to relax and sleep. A glider pilot might feel the same need, but could expect a battle raging round him. In an instant he must take up a gun and fight. More, he must be ready as gunner, signalman, infantryman.

It was a daunting expectation, and the more Chatterton thought of it the more convinced he became of the need for army and not RAF attitudes—for intensely disciplined, broadly trained men of high initiative.

In setting out to produce what he called 'the total soldier', Chatterton saw 'bull' and drill as essential steps. If the Air Force laughed at the idea of pukka soldiers flying aircraft, there were ways to make it sit up. One of his favourites was to borrow a Tiger Moth, land 'in the most split-arsed manner' at an RAF station and step out immaculate in parade ground uniform with swagger stick.

By autumn, Horsas were numerous, pilots burgeoning. The shortage was of tow-planes. Only two were required for the first glider operation to be mounted from Britain, and the chosen aircraft, four-engined Halifax bombers, had not been tested before as tugs.

They were picked for their long range, the mission calling for a 500-miles tow to release two Horsas over enemy territory. The project was cloaked in secrecy. The camp buzzed. Victor Miller, a pupil pilot, recalled afterwards that a bushy-moustached staff-sergeant named Strathdee was rumoured to be preparing for something special, along with a Sergeant Doig. Both had been early trainees with the unit, Strathdee the first to solo at Haddenham.

One glider would be flown by them, the other by two special-duty pilots of the Royal Australian Air Force, Pilot Officer Davies and Sergeant Fraser. Long-range towing rehearsals presented problems. Not only was the distance unprecedented as a glider haul, the demand was for a night flight. Night gliding was regarded apprehensively. Little time had been granted for preparations, and the hasty training was plagued with mishaps.

Burdened for long periods, the engines of the Halifaxes overheated. Plans to reduce the load by shedding the glider wheels after take-off caused difficulties. Tug towing lights and towline telephones failed. Led by Squadron Leader A. B. 'Wilkie' Wilkinson, a Ringway 'original' and member of the Imperial College Gliding Club, the tug crews worked on the problems with the glider men. Suddenly, the little force was moved to Skitten, Scotland. There, in the drear hutments of Britain's northernmost airfield, operational orders were at last revealed.

Churchill and his heads of intelligence were disturbed. Informed of German research on an atomic bomb, they had become increasingly concerned through the year by the production of its ingredient 'heavy water' at the Norsk Hydro plant, perched in the mountains near Rjukan, Norway. In March, Britain's Special Operations Executive had dropped an agent with intimate knowledge of the area into Norway, reinforcing him in October with four compatriots and the radio device Rebecca-Eureka, used to guide aircraft from the ground.

Mindful of the German demolitions at Eben Emael, Churchill now planned to land a force by gliders to destroy the plant. This would be met and guided by the agents, who would afterwards lead it through the mountains to neutral Sweden.

The operation called for a glider-load of skilled engineers but, because of the hazards, two teams would set out. The men, volunteers from the airborne forces, were led by sapper officers, Lieutenants D. A. Methuen and A. C. Allen. They had trained strenuously for a task which involved not only a glider flight of several hours, and the sabotage, but an arduous trek through craggy and snow-swept heights.

'Freshman,' the somewhat ominous code-name of the enterprise, took place on the night of 19 November 1942, exactly a month after the last four agents had entered Norway. Take-off was due in daylight, but further problems with lights and communications delayed the machines until dark. Given the choice of leaving or waiting another day, the glider pilots opted to go ahead.

At 17.50 Wilkinson's Halifax, with Strathdee's glider, hauled into a soup of rain and unbroken cloud. Twenty minutes later, the second tug, flown by a Canadian, Flight Lieutenant Parkinson, with Davies flying the glider, climbed after them. Vision through the streaming Horsa windscreens was minimal. In cloud, the Halifaxes became ghosts, their lights obscured. The strain on towlines was perilous. But the forecast was for clear skies, a good moon over Norway, and they left the ground staff at Skitten with fingers crossed.

Hours passed heavily at the Scottish base.

Ahead of the combinations stretched 400 miles of sea, another hundred of mountains. Fuel reserves in the tugs would be marginal.

Then, at 23.41, the anxious monitors received a faint signal from one Halifax requesting a home bearing. At 23.55, a terse report indicated that a glider was in the sea, a confusing message since radio intersection placed the transmission over Norway, southwest of Rjukan. Something was wrong—how badly, was not known.

In the early hours of the 20th, Wilkinson's Halifax touched down at Skitten with grim news. Contrary to prediction, the clouds had remained thick, but by good use of the gaps Wilkinson had hauled Strathdee above them, crossing Norway at more than 10,000 ft. Then, disasterously, the Rebecca-Eureka failed. The waiting agents heard the Halifax, but snow had rendered the landing zone indistinguishable from the aircraft. Without signals, and barely enough fuel for the return flight, Wilkinson was forced to turn back, glider still in tow. Almost immediately, cloud enveloped them. Ice began to grip them. The towline frosted.

The only escape was by descending through thousands of feet of cloud. For five hours now, Strathdee and Doig had fought to hold their glider behind the Halifax. As they plunged through the vapour, they were still struggling.

Somehow they stayed in tow for another 100-odd miles,

losing height to 3,000 ft, before the line broke. All Wilkinson could do was fly on. Believing himself over sea—in fact, he was at the coast, near Stavanger—he reported the glider lost.

Alone and helpless, Strathdee and his passengers were suspended in mist which turned, as they sank through it, to smothering snow. Below lay Lyse Fjord and the heights of Fylesdalen, where at last they crashed. Most, including Strathdee and Doig, were killed. Four survivors, badly injured, were borne to hospital. Hitler had recently ordered the summary execution of prisoners taken while on sabotage missions, and a German doctor, on Gestapo instructions, forthwith poisoned them.

Unlike Wilkinson, the combination of Parkinson and Davies reached Norway flying low, beneath the cloud base. Crossing the coast south of Stavanger, they had turned for Rjukan when the mountains clawed them from the sky near Helleland. The crash killed all in the Halifax, but most of the glider men survived, to be captured and swiftly shot.

Ultimately, the hydro plant was sabotaged by agents. Meanwhile, Britain's gliders had made a valiant but tragic start. Disaster of a greater magnitude lay ahead.

While Strathdee and his ill-fated comrades hung over Norway, Allied troops were streaming ashore in Morocco to complete the demise of Rommel in North Africa and threaten the so-called 'soft underbelly' of Hitler's Europe. When the 1st Airborne Division was ordered from Britain to join them under General Dwight D. Eisenhower, about 500 of Chatterton's glider pilots had flown Horsas, but few had any experience outside flying school.

On average, they had notched about eight hours of glider flying in six months. This had not included night landings, and few were rated experienced as day pilots. None had flown in action, or reached even the operational training stage. Indeed, as Chatterton protested to his superiors, they were 'totally unfit for operations'. In vain he argued the case for completing their training before they went abroad.

To his frustration, Browning, with whom he had established a close *rapport*, had been succeeded as chief at 1st Airborne by the former commander of the glider landing troops, Brigadier (soon to be Major-General) 'Hoppy' Hopkinson, a small bustling man with wavy black hair and urgent ambitions for his new command. Chatterton was to detail two companies of glider pilots, two to three hundred men, for Africa and proceed there with the first of them.

At Algiers, he encountered Hopkinson in eager mood. 'Well, George,' enthused Hopkinson, 'I've a very interesting operation for you to study.'

Three months earlier, it transpired, Churchill and Roosevelt had approved the invasion of Sicily as a preliminary to wrenching Italy from the Fascist grip. General Montgomery's Eighth Army was to land near Syracuse on the island's east coast; General Patton's Seventh Army, with the American 82nd Airborne Division, on the south coast. Now Hopkinson was telling Chatterton that Montgomery had agreed to use gliders in a night landing ahead of the main forces. D-day would be 10 July.

It staggered Chatterton. Uncomfortably, it was 1 April, All Fools' Day. He glanced at Hopkinson's aerial photographs of the Sicilian coast: rocky outcrops, cliffs, small fields enclosed by stone walls. With the added perils of a night flight, the operation bore an unhealthy resemblance to the glider attack on Crete. Chatterton would have three months in which to prepare for it. At that moment he had neither gliders nor towing planes in Africa. The US Air Force, Hopkinson assured him, would provide both.

'American gliders?'

'Yes,' said Hopkinson, 'what difference will that make?'

The American glider was the Waco. Until Eben Emael, US commanders, like the British, had seen no military value in glider flying. Then, in 1941, they had moved urgently. General Henry H. Arnold, Chief of the Army Air Force, had launched the programme. Co-ordinated by an American soaring expert, Lewin Barringer, it devolved primarily on the

Waco CG4, which the British called the Hadrian. It was a 15-man high-wing aircraft with wooden wings and steel-framed fuselage, produced in mass at the Ford factories.

The Waco flew well but tended to float further than the Horsa when landing—too far for safety when space was tight. Space in Sicily was likely to be very tight. Moreover, to convert raw pilots from one plane to another in a few weeks, then send them into action, was to ask for trouble. But Hopkinson was adamant. When Chatterton demurred, he was given half an hour to accept the scheme or relinquish command of the glider mission.

In that event, control of the operation must pass to an officer without proper experience, for only Chatterton had the flying background to prepare the glider pilots. As he saw it, it was his duty to 'stand by the men, despite the fact that I considered the plan mad'.

Now the Wacos, whose whereabouts was lost amid the vast quantities of equipment shipped to Africa, had to be tracked down. They were found 200 miles to the west, at Oran, dismembered and strewn about the airfield in large crates. Consulting the handbooks, the glider pilots began building the craft themselves, living in the crates as they emptied them. With Chatterton they slogged in the fierce heat. Time was short. They had yet to get the hang of the strange planes and ferry them 600 miles east to take-off strips in Tunisia, facing Sicily.

Another problem was posed by the Waco's size. Unlike the Horsa, which could lift a jeep and a light gun, the Waco could take one or the other, but not both. Unless the gliders landed safely in pairs—a by no means probable eventuality in the dark—the guns would be immobile, useless to the airborne force. At least a score of Horsas, it was agreed, would be needed to supplement the Waco fleet. But shipping space from England was unavailable, and the ferry flight—quite apart from its dangers—was 300 miles longer than the accepted maximum range of 1,000 miles for a Halifax-Horsa tow. In all, the Sicily scheme raised daunting obstacles.

3

Flight of the Buzzard

Spruced for a 36-hour leave to London, Staff-Sergeant Gordon Jenks paused to watch a Halifax leave Holmsley South airfield for Hurn, Bournemouth, to pick up a Horsa there. Two of his fellow glider pilots were aboard the plane. As his gaze followed it, fumes began to stream from a port engine and, with a terrific explosion, the machine disappeared in a pall of smoke. There were no survivors.

Later, Jenks, who had once played the trumpet in a dance band, was asked by an RAF sergeant if he would play the Last Post and Long Reveille at the funeral of the crew and his dead comrades. It was an experience he would not forget. RAF and glider pilots stood in silent ranks by the fresh graves as the coffins rested.

'They fired three volleys and I started to play. Never had I played with so much feeling as at that moment.' Birds were singing, an aircraft droning overhead, and Jenks noticed that the relatives of the victims were softly weeping. For the first time he was conscious of the bond that had formed, despite disparate attitudes, between the crews of the tugs and the glider men.

A few days later, in early summer, glider pilot Jenks was briefed at Portreath, Cornwall, with a number of his friends, for an astounding trip. They were to fly three new Horsas to Africa. He shared his misgivings with the other men. In the group was a sandy-haired sergeant named Nigel Brown. Brown remembers his near-disbelief when he heard the plan. 'We were to be hauled non-stop to a place called Salé in Morocco, the whole flight over water, the first three hours at wave-top height. We would be flying, if we made it, up to ten hours, three pilots to a glider to ease shifts. A few weeks earlier the authorities had ruled the flight impossible.'

Undeterred by official estimates, tug command had tested the absolute tow-flight endurance of a Halifax. Squadron Leader Wilkinson, the 'Freshman' survivor, had begun the trials. For a whole day he had cruised over England with a Horsa behind him, keeping close to base as his tanks drained. By evening he had clocked 1,500 air miles, landing with a small reserve of gasoline. The flight to Africa was feasible—but on harsh terms.

Extra tanks had been fitted in the bomb bays of his aircraft to give the range. Until they emptied, loss of an engine would be disasterous, for the load exceeded three-motor capability. Moreover, a heavy landing could mean the plane bursting into flames, the fate of three Halifaxes in further tests.

To reduce drag, the glider had to jettison its undercarriage after take-off and land without wheels. And, since the flight was inconceivable in darkness, it meant passing in broad daylight within 100 miles of Luftwaffe bases near the French coast. It also meant keeping below 500 ft to miss radar scans.

As Brown remembers it: 'Packs of Ju 88s could be expected over Biscay. They had shot down several British planes in that area. If attacked, were to go into low-tow to give the Halifax gunners a clear field. The fact was that neither tug nor glider was likely to survive an attack in combination, so the Horsa would have to cast off and ditch.' The prospect was unenviable. According to the Air Ministry, a Horsa could not be ditched successfully. Calculations showed that the nose would break in and the glider be deluged immediately.

Fatalistically, the crews emplaned. In all, an attempt was to be made to get some 30 Horsas to Chatterton. 'Turkey Buzzard,' as the operation was called, was inaugurated by Major Alisdair Cooper, a pilot of unassuming fortitude who had joined the regiment as adjutant. With him as the first glider lifted from the clifftops of Portreath were Sergeants Hall and Antonopoulos. They rose into forbidding black cumulus and Jenks, in the second Horsa, was glad to see them climb safely from the aerodrome.

Beside Jenks, in his own glider, was Percy Attwood, a calm pipe-smoking sergeant; behind them, their Cockney pal, Harry Flynn. As they took off there was a violent bump and the glider began to swing erratically behind its tug. Part of the undercarriage, which should have dropped free as they rose, had shot upwards and stuck in the starboard wing. Only with controls hard to port, and by brute strength, could Jenks and Attwood control the craft. It was a poor beginning to a flight of 1,300 miles.

They had decided on hourly turns of flying, but after 15 minutes Attwood, who had taken the first stint, was so hard-worked fighting the unbalanced glider that they settled for 30-minute shifts. Before the first elapsed, the clouds had lowered to an angry-looking sea, the Halifax was invisible and they were being tossed roughly on the line's end. Jenks, relieving Attwood at the controls, felt 'like a tenderfoot cowboy put on a bucking bronco for the first time'.

Brown's glider was in the same cloud. 'The tug simply disappeared. I could just about make out the V in the towrope,' he recalls, 'but where the Halifax was I couldn't tell. I didn't think we would get far. Any moment I expected the line to snap, or be shredded on the tug's propeller blades. It was terribly quiet in the cockpit. Suddenly, the radio silence was broken to say one of the gliders was going down.' It was Cooper's. His line had snapped.

Brown's line, had he known it, was sagging perilously behind his own tug. Emerging from cloud into clear air, he found himself practically on top of the Halifax. Carefully, the glider was teased back to rightful place.

Cooper, flying free, broke cloud at about 100 ft and prepared to ditch. As forecast, the nose caved in as the glider struck the water, and the body filled. With Hall and Antonopoulos, Cooper gained their rubber dinghy and waited for the plane to sink. Twelve hours later, when a rescue vessel reached them, the glider was still afloat. The fuselage had submerged but the wings stayed on the surface supporting it—a portent for survival in the weeks ahead.

Two combinations were still flying. Jenks had issued from cloud into dazzling sun to see no sign of the Halifax ahead of him. At last, he spotted it. The tug was at least 50 ft below the Horsa. With the help of its pilot, Flight Lieutenant 'Buster' Briggs, Jenks regained station without breaking the towline.

The glider was flying less erratically. Handing the controls to Flynn, Jenks went back into the fuselage, removed his sweat-sodden clothing and donned African uniform. Through a porthole, he examined the damaged wing. What he saw did not encourage him. Part of the wheel was in the flaps, so they could not be used to control the landing. A parachute had been fitted to the undercarriage to float it to the ground when it was jettisoned. This, Jenks saw, was still attached to them, threatening to ripple open with results he did not like to contemplate.

Nothing could be done. Rummaging among the luggage, Jenks unpacked his trumpet. He spent the remainder of his off-duty shift playing it.

Several hours out from England the cloud began to thin and then disappeared. The tension eased. No longer in danger of attack from France, the pilots sat back eating chocolate and taking drinks. Lisbon slid beneath the port wing; the sun blazed. Stripping to the waist, they donned dark glasses and joked by phone with the rear-gunner of the Halifax. They had been flying for ten hours when the long coast of Africa appeared ahead.

In Brown's Horsa, all three pilots crammed the cockpit to

peer through scalding perspex. They saw Rabat, gleaming white against tawny sands, and Salé airstrip not far away. There was a sense of history in the aircraft. Americans and Moroccans were peering up, running to see the first gliders over towed from England to Africa.

The damaged ship led the way in. Flynn was handling it, Jenks standing in the doorway to the fuselage. They had released at 600 ft, making a gentle turn to approach the runway without flaps. It was, Jenks thought, tidy if overfast. Then, abruptly, the snarled chute whipped open, jerking the wheel from the starboard wing. It hit the tailplane and, with a crack, the chute caught the tailfin.

At 80 mph, the Horsa spun through 90 degrees, screeching, tearing the runway mesh. With a lurch it subsided in sandy scrub and three shaken but grinning sergeants emerged from it. Only when Brown's glider slid to a perfect halt were the spectators convinced that Flynn's landing was not par for Britain's glider men.

Back in England, Jenks prepared for his second 'Turkey Buzzard' run with new companions: Sergeants Charlie Coombs and Douglas Hatton. Coombs, formerly a military policeman, was a strapping man; Hatton, a rubicund Lancastrian. They had been flying about four hours when the Halifax went into a steep dive. In his earphones, Jenks could hear the tug crew shouting, but his own urgent inquiry brought no reply. The tug pilot had put his plane on automatic control while he stretched his legs. The device had failed. They pulled out at the last moment and skimmed the waves.

Next morning, Jenks watched the Halifax take off from Salé with 2,400 gallons of high-octane fuel aboard for the return trip. In a repetition of the disaster at Holmsley South, smoke poured from an engine, the aircraft lost height and crashed in flames. There was one survivor. The rear turret was thrown clear on impact and the gunner lived.

Others met trouble on future trips. Flynn's second flight

was ill-fated. Nine Ju 88s attacked and shot down the combination over the Bay of Biscay. Flynn was picked up by a destroyer after several hours. Hall and Antonopoulos hit the water again a week after their first ditching, this time intercepted by the Luftwaffe off Cape Finisterre. The third member of their crew, glider pilot Paddy Conway, had stuck a rifle through one of the ports in the aircraft and taken pot-shots. After a brave attempt to evade the enemy, the Halifax captain was compelled to ask Antonopoulos to cast off.

The ditched glider crew spent eleven days and nights in a constantly deflating and swamped dinghy, Conway often unconscious and delirious. At one point they watched another Halifax-Horsa combination heading south to Salé, but were not spotted. With little water, and insufficient saliva to dissolve food tablets, they grew too weak to paddle. Somehow Antonopoulos, a tough pilot of Greek origin, contrived to pump the bellows every two hours.

'My heart would pound and my ears felt as if they were going to burst.' The glare had almost blinded him. On the tenth day, another plane appeared without sighting them. Then, on the eleventh, wraithed in sea mist, they heard a boat's motor and raised their rescue-whistles to parched lips. It was a Spanish trawler. They had drifted to within 20 miles of Oporto, Portugal.

Their tug, they learned later, had escaped the enemy. After shooting down one of its attackers, it had reached cloud, arriving at Salé with 36 cannon-shell hits on it.

The efforts of the tug crews were tireless in 'Turkey Buzzard'. One Halifax was 300 miles out from Cornwall at sea level when an engine failed. With everything possible jettisoned, the pilot nursed the glider back to base on less power than ought, by rights, to have supported the tug alone. Taking off again, he flew the Horsa to Africa but was lost with his crew on the way home. Another Halifax crew flew for 37 hours without rest. Six days later, they made another haul. On their fourth, they disappeared, probably shot down, with the glider crew.

At Salé, the Air Force fliers had to do their own maintenance. Instead of sleeping, they worked through the night, returning to England the next day. There were no spare crews or tug planes. At the conclusion of the epic, by mid-June, 27 Horsas had been delivered to Africa, four lost.

That was not the end of the long haul. The craft had now to be flown to Algeria and, with the Wacos, ferried to the Tunisian invasion strips. It meant crossing the high spine of North Africa, from the Rif to the Hoona Mountains, at up to 9,000 ft. As a spectacle, the flight enthralled. To port stretched the sapphire coast of the Phoenicians; to starboard, the wild majesty of the Sahara. Somewhere ahead, on the lands of lost Carthage, Hannibal had fought Scipio. But, as a glider tow, it had scant appeal.

In the furnace of the day, air turbulence above the heights could plunge an aircraft a thousand feet to impale it on jagged peaks. Climbing to a safe altitude with a Horsa involved 90 minutes of laboured flight for a tug whose engines heated to alarming temperatures. The alternative, starting when the sun was low and threading the valleys of the *Haute Plateau*, meant straining for hours into blinding rays.

Many of the hastily assembled Wacos had not been test-flown. Stories of grisly mishaps circulated, one concerning a craft with crossed control lines which zoomed straight into a loop and fell on its back. The tail section of a Waco came off in mid-air, casting its occupants to their death.

None of Chatterton's pilots, with the exception of the group which had flown the Horsas from England, had made a flight of more than an hour's duration. After a single circuit of the airfield to get the feel of the new ships, they swung east. Staff-Sergeant Victor Miller had breakfasted in an American mess on frankfurter. The sky was rough and he felt queasy. His tug was an Albemarle, a twin-engined British bomber rejected by most branches of the Air Force for combat purposes. A number of Albemarles had been sent to Africa to serve as glider tugs.

Miller recalls his wretchedness as the involutions of the

Atlas passed below, the Albemarle rising and falling in a seesaw motion the glider and his stomach began to emulate. Before volunteering to fly gliders he had been employed on army survey duties, measuring Kentish fields to assess their proneness to German glider landings. It had seemed less thrilling than the chance to pilot his own aircraft. Now, belly churning, he had doubts.

Other combinations were struggling. The sun was molten, the cabin of each glider a hothouse. Increasingly, the turbulence jolted them. With each air pocket, the scorched peaks below loomed frighteningly, broken only by ravines and parched river-beds. Miller's tug captain had engine problems. 'He was losing power. We were getting closer and closer to the mountains. Without warning, the Albemarle would drop like a stone, leaving us dangling as it strove to climb again. Finally, it was clear it was not going to make it unless we cast off.'

Somewhere in the Atlas, Miller's glider flopped amid giant ant-hills, the only shade for its occupants under the ship's wings. The pilots were found by the French Foreign Legion and emplaned again. The assault on Sicily was a fortnight away now, tug crews flying seven hours a day to complete the move. One pilot survived six engine failures due to the heat on the trips he made. Five tow-planes ran out of fuel. Amazingly, all but ten of 350 gliders arrived in good shape.

Miller turned up a day before the operation. The region he surveyed had a graveyard atmosphere, sprinkled with the ruins of antiquity and the desert war. Once, the eastern coast of Tunisia, dominating the Sicilian narrows and the Tarshish trade, had been prosperous. Now, it was arid waste. Dried-out saltings stretched like white scars in a dustscape specked with sketchy aloes and prickly pear.

On the bleak strips, air crews and glider troops camped in pup-tents, the few Nissen-huts taken as ops. rooms. Chubby Dakotas of the American troop carrier force, the bulk of the towing fleet, squatted in dusty lines. Near one strip, a plume of smoke from a crashed Albemarle smudged the heavens.

Earlier, an ammunition dump had made a larger pall, exploding when a scrub fire enveloped it. Everyone, as Miller recalled it, had a dazed look. That it was the eve of their first assault, the biggest glider lift by any nation at that time, seemed scarcely possible.

4

To Syracuse

Twenty-four hours before lift-off Chatterton walked to the shore near the airstrip to be alone. The forecast was for calm weather, but the white heads on the rollers denoted wind. 'Ladbroke,' as the Sicily assault was designated, remained for him a flawed plan.

Seven hours before the main seaborne landing on Sicily the gliders were to pitch near Syracuse, on the southeast coast, and secure the approaches to that city. Among these, the Ponte Grande, a short distance from the harbour, would provide Montgomery's 5th Division with a vital bridge across two obstacles, a canal and river, on its drive north.

Three air landing zones had been selected. Here, the force of some 130 gliders from Tunisia was to disgorge 1,200 men of the 1st Airlanding Brigade, this composed of units from several British regiments together with guns and jeeps. Most of the glider pilots would be British, though a few Americans had volunteered to make up numbers. On the other hand, the majority of tow-planes and their crews were American.

A prime objection to the scheme was the night flight. For all but its initial stage, the 300-mile haul to Sicily would be in dusk or darkness. Despite Chatterton's best efforts to provide last-minute training on the Wacos, most of the pilots had flown them for not much more than four hours, only about an hour at night. None had flown an attack before. Nor had the American air crews seen action.

Trained for transport duties, the Americans flew unarmed and unarmoured Dakotas lacking the basic protection of self-sealing tanks. In these planes they were now required to trundle for hours over water with the gliders, at risk to interception, and release their gliders on a hostile coast. In darkness, the gliders had to pinpoint landing areas in terrain Chatterton regarded as unsuitable even for day landings.

Walking back to his tent, he could only hope the wind would drop. Next evening, 9 July, as he drove to his glider, it was still strong. Off shore, waves were leaping as pilots made their final checks. Staff-Sergeants Brown and Galpin, veterans of 'Turkey Buzzard', inspected the Horsa they would fly. Crammed in its fuselage, rather like travellers in a London 'Tube', Staffordshire infantrymen sat patiently. With them were mortars and, to Brown's discomfort, a 'Bangalore torpedo'—a weapon that would engulf them in flaming phosphorous if its charge were hit.

Glider pilot Captain Boucher-Giles flew with Miller. They were to land a 6-pounder anti-tank gun and its crew. Miller had missed the briefing. 'All I'd been shown was a night map with a field marked on it near Syracuse. I had no idea who we might meet.'

At 22, dark and debonair, he was not dismayed. 'I reckoned those who had planned it must know their job.'

It was six o'clock in the evening when Chatterton gave the thumbs-up and held his Waco down the runway behind its Dakota tug. Earlier, Peter May, the wing commander in charge of the British tow-planes, had asked if he could have Chatterton's admired chukka boots if the glider officer did not return. 'Of course,' Chatterton had told him, 'just ask my batman.' Now, as they gained speed, the Dakota vanished in its own dust, reappearing as they gained height. Circling, the leading combinations waited for the others to lift off. It was still bumpy from the heat of the day, and the glider pilots were soon sweating as they wrestled with their controls. Captain Peter Harding, beside Chatterton, was airsick.

Already barely airborne, some pilots were in difficulty. Brown and Galpin had been flying a few minutes when an engine on their Halifax tug overheated and its pilot, Flight Lieutenant Tommy Grant, banked steeply to regain the strip. The glider men were about to release when the engine picked up and they set off again. Some released immediately. In one, a jeep had bucked its mooring and threatened to plunge through the flimsy fuselage. The pilot of another saw an engine of his tug ablaze. A number of the hastily assembled ships proved unairworthy. The crews, where possible, transferred to spare planes.

The rest streamed east as the light waned. Chatterton, with time to glance astern, was exhilarated by the sight of the air armada. The Dakotas flew in echelons of four, leader navigating; the all-British combinations, independently. To avoid radar detection they hugged the wavetops. Glider pilots could see spume scudding over the tugs ahead.

Staff-Sergeant Mills, at the controls of one glider, was disturbed by the sight of unfamiliar and distant aircraft, but they turned out to be Mustangs and flew off. Mills saw some ships. By the size of the waves beside them he judged the wind to be strengthening, despite which his glider was handling well. Looking back at the troops he carried, he noticed they were munching barley-sugar—rather quietly, it occurred to him. The passengers in Miller's glider were swigging whisky. They seemed cheerful, and Miller took a turn at the whisky bottle.

They were flying due east. At Malta, which should appear after two to three hours aloft, they would bear north some hundred miles to Cape Passero, southeastern Sicily, and Syracuse. Dusk and the wind, which was increasing, brought problems. Already, arms were aching from holding the gliders behind the tugs, and soon straining through the gloom made eyes and heads throb. In the shadowy Dakota echelons, pilots switched on rear-facing wing lights, exhausts glowed. It was easy to lose position. Chatterton, watching the lights ahead, saw them slide disconcertingly to starboard of him. Suddenly, by the moon's gleam, he saw he was flying side-by-side with his own tug. Hitting rudder and aileron, he jockeyed back.

Another glider crew, McMillen and Halsall, found themselves following an unlit Dakota. An electrical fault had doused its lights. Grabbing an axe from his glider troops, Major McMillen hacked a panel from the windscreen. Air rushed in with gale ferocity, but without the intervening perspex he could just see the white star on the Dakota's wing.

Mills had been flying three hours when a beacon of searchlights loomed ahead. It was Malta, six beams raised as prearranged to guide the glider fleet. 'We were dead on course. We approached the island low, and in the strange artificial half light I could see the preceding combinations banking into the turn to bring them on course for Sicily.'

Chatterton made out the cliffs of the island and felt relieved. So far, so good. Now they would ascend steadily to their release height. The waves, as they climbed, looked less menacing. There was a half-moon.

Back on the Tunisian strips, the ground staff waited, flares prepared for the returning tugs. The small group of Halifaxes, being the fastest, were expected first and, indeed, began arriving soon after midnight. Grant reported compass and automatic pilot failures in his own plane. One Halifax came back on three engines; the tanks of the Albemarles were empty. But they were safe.

At the British base, all tugs were home before the last landing flare petered and blew out.

News from the American strips was as heartening. The Dakotas were roaring back. Some reported icing problems; a few touched down at distant airfields, one as far off as Tripoli. Nevertheless, by daylight the checkboards balanced. Every tug had survived. It seemed too good to be true. Word of the gliders had yet to come.

As Malta had dwindled, the moon dimmed, the wind rose. Mills's ship began to buck in the turbulence, and he hoped the troops aboard would not arrive over Sicily airsick. McMillen's Waco, wind lashing through the hole in its canopy, ploughed through darkness so impenetrable that the hours he had spent studying air photos seemed pointless. Landmarks would be invisible. Captain Smith, his Dakota pilot, strained anxious eyes. Like other tug pilots, he had his work cut out avoiding collision with the many aircraft groping for Cape Passero.

Some climbed, some dived or veered sharply to miss gliders and tugs which loomed in front of them. Some were blown off course by the high wind. Most were aiming for a release height of 1,800 ft, but a number flew higher to dodge the traffic, or in the belief that the gliders would have more chance to find their targets from greater altitude. In many cases, to add confusion, communications between tug and glider were minimal. The stretching of nylon towlines had disconnected the phone wires attached to them. In Miller's glider, the phone had gone dead soon after take-off. Mills had lost communication with his tug before Malta.

Upwards of a quarter of the combinations, as they reached the coast of Sicily, lacked sound.

McMillen's intercom was working, but brought scant comfort. In the headphones he could hear Smith declaring himself lost. Anti-aircraft fire had sprung up from two points and the American, penetrating both barrages, suggested the first might be from Syracuse and that they should turn back. Imperturbably, the Dakota pilot threaded the shell-bursts a second time. Fearful he might yet decide on a third run, McMillen prepared to cast off from him.

Around them, combinations were milling in a blind swarm. How far they were from shore, how far the gliders would sail, was problematical. The gusts were incalculable. Uncertainly, the tugs scattered their burdens above the black sea. As Chatterton reached for his release lever he told Harding, 'I can't see a damned thing'. He was not alone. At least half his pilots could not see the coastline; almost none could identify their landing zones.

Searchlights and tracer appeared as they strained their eyes. At less than 200 ft, Chatterton saw land—a cliff face which seemed to rush at him—and he pulled the glider into a climbing turn. Almost at once enemy fire hit a wing and the tip crumbled. Then the Waco was in the sea. With its passengers, who included Brigadier 'Pip' Hicks and his staff of the 1st Airlanding Brigade, Chatterton swam ashore as a machine-gun opened up at them. Despondent and unarmed, he lay on the beach watching his pilots picked out by the searchlights above the waves.

One, Staff-Sergeant Ellis, was forced to ditch not far from shore. Stripping, he set out to test the distance to the beach on behalf of the glider troops clinging to the floating plane. It was a fair swim and, having rested, he started back to advise the others. Unaware of the strong current, Ellis heaved himself on a waterlogged wing to find it belonged to another glider. He never regained his own craft. Back ashore, he was captured, still naked, by an armed patrol.

Many gliders came down much further from Sicily. Mills, estimating the distance by the searchlights, reckoned he was two miles from land when he ran out of air. Steering by the white crests of the waves, he splashed down and was immediately deluged in the cockpit. He grabbed a rifle and smashed the roof out. The sea was rough, but somehow, arms linked on the pitching wing, Mills and the glider troops survived for four hours, until a vessel with the incoming seaborne force picked them up.

They were lucky. Of 68 gliders to land at sea that night, most disappeared without trace, pilots and troops drowned. Some had parted from their tugs too far from shore to have any chance of reaching land; others might have made it but for the strength of the off-shore wind. Of the original fleet, 122 gliders had approached Sicily. Fifty-four remained to face the land hazards foreseen by Chatterton.

McMillen thanked Smith for the ride before he cast off.

Away from the Dakota, the blast through his broken windscreen was less severe. Circling, he swirled down through the night towards the unknown. A fire was burning. What or where it was he did not know, but it was his only landmark and he steered for it. Halsall was reading the altitude aloud to him: 'Four hundred . . . three hundred . . . two hundred feet . . .'

Suddenly, black crowns of trees were ahead and McMillen heaved back. The Waco lifted. He put the nose down, regaining speed, then flattened out. The last he knew of the flight was Halsall shouting, 'Nought feet, eighty-five miles an hour,' then impact. He lost consciousness. When he came round, the tubular framework of the cabin was wrapped about him. Halsall, slumped on the panel, was outlined against the flames they had followed in their descent. The fire was another glider burning in a tomato field.

Its pilot, Captain Alec Dale, had led the survivors from the field when he heard the whistle of a Waco descending fast. Diving for cover, he chose the bole of the very tree McMillen hit. For some moments Dale waited dazedly for signs of life in the wrecked plane. When none was evident, he approached apprehensively in time to catch McMillen as he lurched out. Halsall was concussed, the glider troops stunned but not badly hurt. Supporting McMillen, whose foot was injured, they headed in the presumed direction of the canal bridge, intermittent explosions directing them.

Gliders were falling over many miles. One, hit on the wing, spiralled down like a shot bird. Another, crashing on the rocky beach, was set ablaze by an incendiary grenade, its pilot pinned by the legs as ammunition began to detonate. Resolved to shoot himself rather than burn to death, he could not find a weapon within reach. 'For God's sake, get me a rifle,' he told his co-pilot. An ammunition box exploded and the co-pilot collapsed, an arm shattered. Struggling to his companion, he contrived to wedge his back under the burning wreckage and lift it an inch or two. Agonizingly, and at the cost of a broken leg, the trapped man wormed from the inferno.

It was his turn to aid the other. Binding a crude tourniquet to his friend's arm, he dragged himself to the sea and started to swim for help, one-legged.

Meanwhile, as Brigadier Hicks crouched with Chatterton beneath the cliff, his deputy, Colonel 'Jonah' Jones, was scrambling from a Waco along the coast. Accompanied by a small staff and the glider pilots, he lay up in a farmyard scheming an attack on a nearby gun post. Troop-packed gliders were still releasing, slipping earthwards. Chatterton was pondering his next move when a boat approached the beach and a party of SAS men jumped from it. Together, they scaled the cliff. Jones, receiving no such reinforcement, led his men against the gun post, hurling hand-grenades.

5

Bridge Party

The engine problem developed by Grant's Halifax on take-off put it well behind the others, and it was already dusk as the trailing Horsa was lost to sight from Africa. Glider pilots Brown and Galpin were not too worried. It was a relief, after the crisis, to be on their way at all, and the Halifax could make up time on the slower tugs. In fact, though they did not spot any Horsas, a few laggard Wacos were in sight before darkness fell.

Delay favoured them. Grant had climbed to 6,000 ft over Cape Passero and, as they followed the coast north, the reception for the earlier gliders pinpointed Syracuse. Their landing zone was the closest to the Ponte Grande, a strip of land a few hundred yards to the west of it. Brown recalled that their release zone, east of the bridge, had been calculated on a low wind velocity.

When Grant suggested that, in view of the rising wind, he should take them nearer than planned they did not demur. So far, they had not been detected by the enemy.

Meanwhile, Miller and Boucher-Giles had approached at 1,800 ft, subjected to spasmodic fire as they ran the coast. Their arrival in the release area was marked by a barrage which reminded Boucher-Giles of the Blackpool lights. The

Albemarle tug bored into it. There was scant discussion. The telephone was faulty; the glider pilots, in Miller's words 'knackered by trying to keep out of the Mediterranean'. They cast off.

'Almost at once there was a bang, then the cabin was bathed in a purplish light.'

In the tenseness of the moment they had forgotten to disconnect the phone cable and the instrument had been snatched through the front of the cockpit by the Albemarle. Moments later, a searchlight homed on them. Doughtily, the tug went down and shot the beam out. Night enveloped them. 'It was pitch black. The moon had gone. Dimly, I could make out the land-mass and fires burning, but we had reached the last few hundred feet before shadowy features appeared below.' When they did, Miller was dismayed to see stout walls and olive groves.

Boucher-Giles was flying, Miller calling the altitude. At 110 ft, they were travelling at 120 mph—much too fast, he thought. Ahead, the zone was crisscrossed with tracer, and gliders burned. Boucher-Giles dared not land in it. Instead, he kept his airbrakes up and sped on, Miller bellowing the speed with increased alarm. A small field appeared. Something grey loomed in the windscreen and Miller, hurled forward, saw a scarlet flash.

When he came to, he remembered the last airspeed reading. They had impacted at 110 mph. He was lying among the controls, while someone groaned in the fuselage. The anti-tank gun had jerked forward, smashing into one of their passengers, Sergeant Hodge. Boucher-Giles was uninjured. Pulling Hodge beneath the wing, he lay there with the other occupants, three men of the Border Regiment, as Miller looked for his sten-gun. He could not find it. Joining the others, he heard bullets flying over them.

For a while they lay listening to the bullets and crumpling gliders. 'You could hear the whistle of the Wacos as they came in, then the thump. Most were crashing.' No one appeared, and without a jeep the gun was useless. Finally, leaving a man with the crippled Hodge, the others set out for the Ponte Grande.

It was getting on for midnight; the bridge several miles away. Miller had no weapon, but after a while they ran into a band of South Staffordshire glider men, one of whom gave him a hand-grenade. He lost it diving for cover as they were pinned by fire again. For the naturally jaunty Miller, it was becoming a depressing mission. 'At that time, I didn't know the half of it.'

South of Syracuse, a rocky snout, Cap Murro di Porco, jutted into the Ionian Sea. As Brown and Galpin released their Horsa they could just see the dim shape of the promontory far below. Setting course for the target on their compass, they flew by it. In the back, the glider troops braced themselves.

They were still undetected when the moon appeared, revealing Syracuse directly under them. Galpin swung the ship southwest towards where he imagined the bridge lay. Now, by the improved light, he could make out the area they had studied on the night maps. At 2,000 ft, a searchlight caught them and tracer flew up. Galpin dived and banked. The shaft clung to them. Evasive action had taken them to sea again, bathed in light.

Watching 20 mm tracer approaching them, Brown thought of the explosives in the fuselage. They dived again. The searchlight stuck to them. Ahead, parallel waters, the canal and river, ran inland to the Ponte Grande and the field beside it. Flying low, they followed the banks, eyes straining to pick out the landing place. Now the searchlight, almost flat, was silvering bridge girders and unwelcome walls. Raising the glider's nose, Galpin rammed on full flaps and put the ship down. Apart from a wheel lost in a ditch, there was little damage.

The commander of the glider troops, Lieutenant Withers, had sprained an ankle, the rest were unharmed. Since no one attacked them, the glider pilots celebrated with a tot of Scotch. They scarcely knew how unique they were. Of the entire fleet, a handful had landed as planned that night, only one other glider dropping at the Ponte Grande. That crashed, exploding its phosphorus bombs.

It pitched in the canal bank. Brown, approaching, was appalled by the sickening mess. One man was still alive, and they gave him a shot of morphia. The other occupants were beyond help, incinerated as the 'Bangalore torpedo' flared.

Moving off, Withers and his glider men—South Staffordshires—seized the bridge and prepared to defend their prize. Galpin had nagging doubts. 'We knew our glider should have been among the last to arrive and we made every effort to contact any of our troops in the vicinity, but found none, and I began to imagine we had landed by the wrong bridge.'

That half the gliders were in the sea, the rest scattered up to 25 miles, was unknown to him. Of 1,200 glider troops on the mission, some 500 should by now have been in the bridge area. In fact, one platoon was there, Withers's, and it would be dawn before another 50 or so men got through to them. Barely another 500 were uninjured in any zone.

At first light, Boucher-Giles, with Dale, Miller and their party, approached the bridge. They found its captors under fire, but no major attack had been launched at them. Running a gauntlet of bullets, the new arrivals raised the force in situation to 87. No more were to get through, for the Italians, reinforced by lorry convoy, had soon ringed the area. Their assault in mass produced a savage fight.

The glider pilots had grouped on the south bank. Dale, shinning a tree in the hope of spotting reinforcements, was thrown down as a machine-gun blasted the bark from it. Miller had found a sten on the night march. Crouched in a trench, he was levelling the weapon when an Italian grenade exploded and knocked him out. He came round, plugged with shrapnel, to see the pilot beside him shot between the eyes. Another enemy burst killed the glider man next to Boucher-Giles, ripping the captain's pack and sending his rifle spinning. Eventually, numbers dwindling, the survivors took refuge in a shallow ditch. Here, they held out against repeated attacks before surrendering.

It was barely over before the vanguard of the seaborne troops arrived to release them and retake the bridge. The glider soldiers had left their captors no time to demolish it.

That day, Chatterton, skirmishing forward in seaborne company, met the grim remains of the glider fleet. The planes were everywhere, often macabre in their twisted shapes. One, having struck a treetop, stood on its nose, a jeep still in it. The dead driver of the jeep was in the driving seat. In another, the pilot lay crushed beneath the gun which had smashed the cockpit bulwark. A third had rammed an escarpment. Its fliers had died on impact.

At Ponte Grande, the relatively undamaged Horsa of Brown and Galpin was shadowed by a charred wreck. The explosion in its fuselage had blown the occupants forward, where their bodies lay in a tragic heap. Chatterton was deeply affected by what he saw. The signs spoke of high endeavour in adversity, but also of frightful loss. Three days later, the loss was compounded by a new assault.

The purpose of 'Fustian', planned before the outcome of 'Ladbroke' had been assessed, was to seize a second bridge, the Ponte Primosole, north of Syracuse. This time, the operation was mainly by Dakota-borne British paratroops, but 19 gliders were to follow with anti-tank guns. Eleven Horsas and eight Wacos had been mustered from those unused by the 'Ladbroke' fleet.

Towed by Halifaxes and Albemarles, they took the same course to Malta as their comrades, skirting Syracuse over the Allied invasion convoys. Not only was enemy fire from the coast accurate, warships guarding the sea armada pounded them. German aircraft had bombed the vessels. Tensed for the next attack, naval gunners let fly as the roar of tugs and transports filled the night above.

Recognition signals did not avail. Almost every craft opened fire, all too accurately. Ten Dakotas full of paratroops were shot down, 24 turned back in the confusion, many badly hit. Three British tugs which failed to return to Africa probably fell to 'friendly' guns. Among them was Wilkinson's Halifax. The pioneer of long-haul towing, veteran of the first war mission by British gliders, Norway, was lost to the glider force.

The previous day, his comrade, Peter May, flying a special mission behind enemy lines in Sicily, had not returned. Prematurely, May had taken possession of Chatterton's flying boots. May had worn them on the mission, and died in them.

Now, the 'Fustian' gliders sought their landing zones. A third of the small fleet had not made the coast. Approaching shore at 500 ft, glider pilot Alistair Cooper, the first officer to take off (and ditch) on 'Turkey Buzzard', saw his tug blow up in front of him. He was carrying the commander and headquarters of the operation. All were killed as Cooper desperately struggled to land his craft. Another pilot, Staff-Sergeant White, met such a blaze of fire from the ground that it flood-lit his landing zone. He came down with a stunning crunch 100 yds from the Ponte Primosole and, with co-pilot and passengers, fought to get jeep and gun into action.

One glider, swooping through a hail of bullets, used a cluster of burning haystacks as its flare-path. The pilot ran full-tilt into the only stack that was not in flames. Shaken but uninjured, the crew unloaded their jeep and raced towards the bridge. Before reaching it, they were surrounded and captured by German paratroops who had dropped earlier to defend the area.

Several glider pilots, including a young lieutenant, Thomas, managed to join White's group after landing miles away. As at Syracuse, the bridge was captured by a fraction of the force, which held on until overwhelmed. Again, the bridge was recaptured promptly by seaborne troops. On both occasions, bravery was conspicuous, glider and tug pilots receiving high awards later for their endeavours.

But there could be little doubt the losses, considered with

the small proportion of gliders to land as planned, urged close analysis.

At Primosole, 4 of 19 gliders which left Africa had landed accurately; at Syracuse, 16 of 137, 13 of this number without damage or casualties. It was true that scattered gliders caused alarm and confusion among the enemy, and that Montgomery held the taking of Ponte Grande an important stroke. But had gliders not proved a clumsy means to such useful ends? Only one in every 15 men of the glider force, and none of the guns it carried, had got into the action at Ponte Grande.

Of the rest, 326 men were missing, presumed drowned; another 279 killed or wounded. More than half the glider troops—men of the artillery, Staffordshires, Ulster Rifles, Border Regiment and Ox. and Bucks.—were casualties. Fifty-seven glider pilots had been killed. And that was the operation alone, not the build-up.

Looked at another way, it had taken the effort and losses of 'Turkey Buzzard' and the Atlas haul, months of preparation for some 150 tug crews and 300 glider pilots, all the ground work that went with it, to put less than 90 men on the Ponte Grande and create some scattered skirmishes. On a small scale, Plimosole was the same tale.

In the words of a glider pilot who made the first bridge, 'It was a nightmare, the whole thing'.

General Hopkinson, a brave man who had not flinched from flying with his own troops—he had survived the sea, and later was killed in Italy—described the outcome of the project he had espoused so eagerly in stronger terms. Unprintable, they were directed in the first flush of anguish at the American transport wing. Many glider men, including some of the American volunteers, blamed the Dakota pilots for their inability to reach land. In return, glider pilots were accused of discrepancies.

Some would sustain their bitterness. More, in time, conceded that too much had been expected of all involved. Neither British nor Americans were experienced or properly trained in such an exploit, nor were the latter equipped for it. Their slow, unarmed Dakotas were not combat aircraft. On top of which, adverse weather and visibility, combined with phone failures, understandably confused tug and glider crews.

More fundamentally, gliders were inappropriate at Sicily. They were new and, to the planners of the invasion, seemed handy instruments. But like the Germans who had decided to use them against Crete, they picked the worst situation, a hilly coast, magnifying the German error by choosing a night attack. It had been, as Chatterton expressed it to an American air force colonel, the outcome of 'sheer ignorance'.

Not long afterwards, the air landing men threw a party for Britons and Americans alike in the emotion-charged dust of their Tunisian camp. Ammunition-boxes were filled with flowers, wine produced from bombed villages. Slowly, recriminations changed to mutual condolences; condolences, to stubborn pledges to see it through.

For the Germans, Crete had been the end of assault gliders. For Britain, as America, the Sicilian tragedy was a lesson on the way to glider attacks of undreamed magnitude.

6

Mammoths and Flying Mules

Once, Adolph Hitler had placed faith in a giant glider. Churchill's demand for sky troops raised the problem the Führer had sought to crack: how to support an air landing with tanks and guns? The only answer was Willy Messerschmitt's, but Britain's planners stopped short of the preposterous. Unlike the Me 321, their giant must not need a near-miracle to get it up. Rather, it should be within the towing capability of the strongest tug available when it flew.

That involved speculation both in the glider and bomber field. To add difficulty, the call for swift development precluded the cautious trials normal to unconventional plane design. In more than one sense, the project was a gamble of magnitude.

Named the Hamilcar, after an ancient general who used elephants, Britain's giant was on the drawing-board while Rock's glider force still flew pre-war sporting planes. In fact, its design, by General Aircraft, had been agreed with the glider unit at an early stage, construction beginning at a Birmingham railway carriage works in 1941. If the Hamilcar hardly resembled rolling stock, nor was it much like a warplane in most eyes. Someone reasonably dubbed it 'a whale with wings'.

Of wooden structure, its single wing spanning 110 ft, the ship was designed to lift a load equal to its own weight of seven tons, and swallow a light tank. Alternatively, it might transport two bren-carriers or the equivalent burden in field guns, gun-hauling vehicles and army trucks. These would enter and unload through a hinged nose of huge proportions, travelling in a hull so cavernous that a house-painter's ladder was proposed to enable the pilots to reach their seats above the fuselage.

At tandem controls behind the swing-nose, the pilots were covered by a bullet-proof windshield and protected at the rear by a section of armour-plate. From wheelbase to cockpit, the height was more than 25 ft. In length, the aircraft measured about 70 ft.

The first prototype made was half-scale. Pressed for time, the manufacturers used solid timbers in the structure instead of trimming them, the extra substance standing in for cargo weight. Amenably, the big baby bumbled skywards and behaved itself. But it was short-lived. Approaching the test-ground too low, a pilot lifted the flaps for extra glide and made splinters of the infant ship. In March 1942, the first full-scale Hamilcar rolled out and took the air.

Witnesses in fields and lanes blinked unbelievingly. With its vast wing-span, bulbous prow and barge-like belly, it might have been some great seaplane but for the absence of engines, and for massive wheels abeam the giant hull. Far ahead, linked by a seemingly endless length of sagging rope, the four-engined Halifax bomber was strangely dwarfed. The scale was unreal, but the giant flew. Indeed, to the credit of its designers, it handled beautifully.

It remained to convince the tug crews. Fourteen tons was a formidable weight to pull, and at take-off the margin between flying and stalling was slim. For trials, a Halifax was used with souped-up engines, but soon improved power units gave standard bombers the power required. The first Hamilcar squadron went into training. Flying tanks were a reality.

Apprehensively, their crews learned the technique. Within the glider, the exhaust pipes of the tank were connected to funnels which ejected fumes from the fuselage, so the vehicle could start up in flight. As the Hamilcar approached ground, the pilots were in contact with the tank crew by telephone. The vehicle warmed up in the glide-in then, as the plane stopped, the tank moorings were released and the machine rolled forward. As it did so, the exhaust extensions disconnected and the glider's nose swung open automatically.

An initial problem was the tricky drop between the floor of the glider and its wheelbase. This was overcome by a thoughtful pilot who helpfully opened the taps on the oleo struts of the undercarriage, releasing the oil pressure. Gently, the great glider subsided on its flat bottom.

The first tank-landing exercise proved breathtaking. One of the Hamilcars, overshooting the runway, bounced ponderously into a group of buildings. As it braked in the rubble, its tank was catapulted through the nose at something like the impact speed of 80 mph, to stop 50 yds on the far side of the buildings, topped with dust and bricks. The glider pilots, stranded high above the ruins, were unharmed. So, incredibly, was the driver of the tank, who emerged from his hatch with a begrimed scowl.

Meanwhile, problems of the Horsa were being tackled. Unloading, especially after heavy landings, was often difficult. In Sicily, the doors of Horsas had either jammed on impact or been distorted so jeeps and guns were un-removable. Thirty minutes or more of toil was sometimes entailed in extricating cargo intended for instant use. Back in England, brains were exercised.

An early device on the Horsa was a girdle of cordtex explosive round the rear of the fuselage, by which means the tail section could be blown off if the door failed. It was a drastic measure, liable to set the plane ablaze. In one instance, it blew up everything: glider, jeep and ammunition. New ways were tried.

The tail unit of the Horsa was attached by bolts at the stern bulkhead. Unscrewing them was slower than using cordite but less hazardous, and crews were now supplied with spanners for this purpose. As a variation, the bolts were replaced by quick-release plugs. On the ground, the idea appealed; in the air, the notion of a quick-releasing tail was less attractive to the glider men. Ultimately, the Horsa was equipped with a hinged nose, but this was not yet.

Sicily had shown the perils of mass release without target guides. One scheme to prevent scattered landings involved the use of conspicuously marked gliders to lead the others to the landing zone. If they missed the mark themselves, at least the fleet would ground in a close area—compactness now a cardinal aim of landing technique. Where night flying was essential, it was proposed that a team of parachutists should drop ahead with lamps which would be set out in a T, indicating direction and zone of landing.

Tried in a mass exercise, the plan misfired when the T was marked at variance with wind direction, indicating a down-wind landing. Half the pilots landed as directed, the rest correcting the mistake on their own initiative. Amazingly, no collisions resulted from the shadowy mêlée above the field.

Another scheme, asking nothing of the pilots, was to release miniature Horsas at the enemy. Both the Germans and the Allies had used dummy paratroops to deceive ground forces, and dummy gliders were proposed as a new hoax. The idea was to make silhouette models from plywood, their 4-ft wings constructed to fold in transportation, snapping open when launched from an aeroplane. Tested on Salisbury Plain, a sample batch looked extremely realistic in distant flight. The plan was rejected by the authorities.

Better supported was the concept of snatching gliders off the ground by using low-flying aircraft with long hooks. So far, gliders had been regarded as expendable elements of air assault, though they might survive in good shape. Reclamation by road was ruled out due to cost and the inaccessibility of landing zones. But if gliders could be whisked aloft again by tugs which did not have to touch down, the scope for their employment gained new breadth. They might be used to recover as well as land men.

The idea, reaching Britain's glider force through the experimental aircraft station at Farnborough, Hampshire, had come from across the globe. Its pioneers were unknown until, from the depths of a tropical jungle, came startling news. While commanders in the West digested the verdict of Crete and Sicily, an inspired general in the East was espousing gliders with zest as a mainstay of his campaign.

In 1942, aided by the pro-Axis clique known as the Thirty Comrades, the Japanese had occupied Burma, dominating the land of pagodas from Rangoon on the southern delta north through the rain forests to fabled Mandalay and the hills beyond. Isolated by mountain ranges from India and China, covered for much of its area by dense jungle, Burma presented a daunting face to operations against its occupation force.

The man chosen to harry the Japanese until larger armies could be effective was Orde Charles Wingate, an eccentric and controversial British general whose archaic solar topee crowned what some called military genius, and all agreed was an unorthodox fighting brain. Wingate's forte was the use of small, highly motivated forces deep in hostile territory, 'one fighting man at the heart of the enemy's military machine being worth', as he put it, 'hundreds in forward battle zones'.

Depending heavily on air transport to lift and supply his long-range penetration groups, Wingate, though not an Airborne commander in the formal sense, became the first Allied general to sustain a campaign with air landings, using gliders enthusiastically. They were new to him but, never slow to innovate, he juggled them. The flying group at his disposal, America's 1st Air Commando, was a match for his novel style.

Commanded by two eager pilots, Colonels Philip G. Cochran and John R. Alison, Air Commando was free of preconceptions, prepared for anything. Among its combat and transport crews were 75 volunteers to fly Wacos in the war's most improbable glider theatre. Jungles and mountains spelled disaster for glider pilots. Yet Wingate's most audacious notions hinged on them.

One of these was the jungle stronghold. Remote and inaccessible to the foe except at dire cost, Wingate's projected 'stronghold' was both a base behind the Japanese from which to harass them, and a barb on which they were invited to immolate themselves. It was manned by hardened troops adept at jungle warfare. Landed and supplied by air, they would be lifted out when at length the base became untenable.

Another Wingate concept, the instant airstrip, made the stronghold possible. First located as a rough hole in the jungle, it had to be manned in force before the enemy could intervene. This meant turning scrub into a landing ground for transports almost literally overnight. Somehow, an initial landing of engineers and implements had to be made on the virgin site. At that time, only gliders could fulfil this exacting task.

Cochran's pilots did not land, like the Sicily fliers, into a bullet storm, but they broke most other precepts of glider safety. They flew into unrecconnoitred forest clearings, doomed by an infinity of trees if they missed the mark. They carried loads to raise the hair of more experienced glider men, often flying a third and more overweight. And, overloaded, they often flew in double-tow, two to a single tug. Not surprisingly, many crashed.

With fatalistic verve the Americans responded to Wingate's needs. Everything from prisoners to mules, from boats to bulldozers, was glider-lifted. Curiously, the mules, notorious renegades, were well behaved. Expected to play havoc in the Wacos, they proved indifferent to bumps and jolts, less ruffled than their handlers by glider trips. The troops bore it. If jungle gliding was dangerous, it was better than slogging through rain forests in full kit.

Wingate's first expedition, in 1943, though modest in effect, was encouraging. Next year he mounted his big campaign. High above Mandalay, in the great fork formed by the Irrawaddy and Chindwin rivers, lay the wild and hilly region he intended to penetrate. The aim was to dominate it until relieved by converging Allied armies: Stilwell's from the north, the Chinese Yoke Force from the east, the British 14th Army from the southern zone. Operating from sequestered strongholds, Wingate hoped to clear northern Burma of the Japanese.

Soon, gliders were diving towards the swirling Chindwin with gear to help men across. One Waco, ripping off a wing as it ploughed into moist silt, landed a patrol to destroy an outpost of the enemy. A couple landed men of the Black Watch to booby-trap trails by which the Japanese might approach. Others, whistling over the murky stream, hit the sand with collapsible boats aboard. Typical of many such pinpoint operations, it was a quick success.

Then, early in March, the gliders massed at one of Wingate's Assam bases, Lalaghat, for a major flight. North of Bhamo, on the Irrawaddy flank of the penetration zone, two Wingate 'strongholds' had been planned. To land the first engineers and escort-infantry in the chosen openings, some 80 Wacos were to fly by night in double-tow over frontier heights rising to 7,000 ft. The target clearings were called 'Broadway' and 'Piccadilly'. Hemmed by dense wood, unknown obstacles concealed in their scrubby bottoms, they represented the last challenge in a trip fraught with wild risks.

Pressed by Wingate's requirements, the glider commander had agreed, albeit doubtfully, to loads of 4,500 lbs—750 lbs over the authorised Waco limit. Doggedly, the soldiers dragged even more foodstuffs and arms aboard. Thus, the risks grew. Approaching take-off, the inherent dangers in Wingate's methods were thrown into stark relief.

With half-an-hour to go, Cochran and the general were standing by the gliders when a light aircraft landed and its pilot was rushed to them. He carried a last-minute aerial photograph of 'Piccadilly' showing tree trunks, like basking crocodiles, all over the chosen site. The Japanese had arrived the same day and blocked the ground. It was 'Broadway' or nothing now.

Sixty minutes later, the force reduced by 20 gliders, the engines roared. Four combinations in double-tow, led by Alison, lifted off as a guide team. Laboriously, they inched to the 8,000 ft needed to clear the heights of Manipur, and strained east. Two-and-a-half hours later, in bright moonlight, they saw the gap in the jungle beneath their wings.

Swooping, the guide gliders landed without much damage, to realise very quickly their goodluck. The first had just missed a wallow made by elephants. Ruts were plentiful. Inspecting the tall grass, they found the concealed hulks of old trees—Burmese teak that took centuries to decompose. As men of the King's Regiment fanned into the shadows to guard the place, Alison looked for his radio, intent on warning the others of the peril there. The set was damaged. Cursing, they heard the next Dakotas drone overhead.

In silent sequence, Wacos began to skim the black woods. The first pair missed the obstacles, then the spills began. The next two lost their wheels and, crunching heavily, were joined in disarray by another four. Immovable, they fouled the path of the ninth, which piled straight into them. Dead and maimed men lay inside while succeeding pilots did their best to leapfrog the wreckage. One overshot into the jungle, demolishing the only bulldozer with the force. Still the radio was not repaired.

Back at Lalaghat, a different picture of trouble was evident. Dakotas returning ahead of schedule brought reports of gliders prematurely adrift over hills and woods. In some cases, towlines rotted by the climate had parted; in others, overloading or mountain turbulence had wrenched the gliders from the towing planes. Some were never heard of from that night. A number, landing far from any friendly post, left survivors to trek to safety or end up captured by the enemy. Meanwhile, Lalaghat still knew nothing of the 'Broadway' mess.

Early that morning came the first word. It was the code for 'Emergency—halt further flights'. Hastily, combinations in the air were ordered back to base.

Of some 850 glider troops lifted, rather more than half were now at 'Broadway', enough at least to get the strip cleared. While patrols and lookouts ringed the area, a hundred soldiers with picks and shovels hacked a runway from the rough ground. Through the night and next day they toiled, until 1,600 yds were flattened. Within 24 hours of the first gliders leaving Lalaghat, Dakotas were landing at 'Broadway' in a steady stream. Wingate's brainchild, the 'stronghold', was reality.

The same month similar strips, 'Aberdeen' and 'Chowringhee', were opened by glider landings to west and south. Through them, into the vitals of the foe, poured troops bent on havoc and sabotage. Other Wacos landed patrols astride Japanese supply lines with radios to direct bomber raids.

Already, precious gliders were being recovered by a new technique. Two poles were placed upright in the ground some yards apart, an extension of the towline strung between them. Approaching low, the tug scooped the line from the poles with a trailing hook. To reduce a jolt which could easily bring disaster to both planes, the line from the tug ran out on a progressively-braking drum, which reversed to wind in excess cable once the glider rose. Though tricky, the feat was accomplished many times. Sick men were recovered by glider snatch.

The penetration of Upper Burma proceeded rapidly, undelayed by Wingate's death in an air crash towards the end of March. Next month another stronghold, 'White City', was established and proved deadly to the Japanese thrown at it. When upwards of 1,500 of them had been accounted for, the men there were pulled out. Though setbacks to Stilwell and the relieving armies stripped Wingate's strategy of ultimate fulfilment, the campaign was a triumph of air landing ingenuity, especially glider use. No longer could commanders ignore gliders as war machines.

They could still malign them, and many did, looking back to Crete and Sicily. But others, looking forward, began to wonder if glider fleets might not win battles. Cochran and Alison were convinced of it. As word of their faith spread, General Eisenhower, planning the greatest invasion in human history, appraised his glider resources with new respect.

7

Night-time, Normandy

On the evening of 5 June, 1944, glider pilot John 'Griff' Griffiths, a determined young man who had run away from home at 16 to join up in 1939, wrote a letter to his girl-friend Jean, of Staines, Middlesex. Sticking the envelope, he held it a moment over the mailbox in the sergeants' mess, Harwell aerodrome, then posted it. It might, he knew, be the last he would write—for a while, at least.

It was almost midnight; almost 6 June, the 24 heroic and horrific hours known simply as D-Day in Western History. With Jock Meiklejohn, his co-pilot, Griffiths prepared for the flight ahead. A stocky man, whose useful fists had won him squadron acclaim as a welterweight, he was soon barely recognisable save for his blue eyes. Grenades bulged the pockets of his shapeless flying smock. A land-mine was strapped like a hump on his back. His face was black.

As the sooty face-cream set, smiling or laughing became difficult. He eyed Meiklejohn. The Scot looked more than usually dour in warpaint. They would not, Griffiths supposed, be laughing much that night.

Beside his own Horsa, Major-General Richard Gale, commander of Britain's 6th Airborne Division (in fact, it was the second, called the 6th to mislead the enemy), smoked a last cigarette before boarding. At fields across England, British and American air troops were stepping into gliders or strapping on parachutes. General Donald Pratt of the American 101st Airborne Division mounted a glider adorned with a symbolic No. 1 and the flag of the United States. There were few illusions: losses in 'Neptune', as the airborne operation was coded, would be heavy—up to 80 per cent by some forecasts. Burdened with fearful responsibility, Eisenhower shuddered as the planes left.

D-Day was minutes old as the main flights climbed from England. It was cloudy and very dark. At the last moment, someone had yanked open the door of Griffiths's Horsa and begged a lift. The man was an army doctor. His own glider had been grounded and he lugged a heavy load with him. The pilots jibbed. Already they carried a jeep, an anti-tank gun and six men. The newcomer would overweight them. He waved a bottle of brandy. They took him on.

Staff-Sergeant Griffiths took the ship up. It responded sluggishly, yawing in the squalls which almost blinded him. In 20-minute stints, the pilots took turns to dog the Albemarle. Below, the Channel was cloaked in murk. They knew precisely the nature of the bulwarks there.

Frantic to consolidate the bondage of conquered Europe, the Führer had drafted thousands of slave labourers to the coast, denuding the Continent of steel and concrete to build his bastion. Even the Maginot and Siegfried Lines had been cannibalised. Half a million men had toiled into summer completing the vast blockhouses and gun turrets which dominated the sea approaches. Rommel, commanding German forces on the French coast, had added trimmings.

Beneath the waves lurked boat-killers: saw-toothed stakes and girders, explosive charges, deadly booby-traps specially designed by the field-marshal. Behind them, Rommel's troops peered ceaselessly from their armoured holds, guns trained on the barbed-wire coiling from beach to promontory. Inland, forests of poles ('Rommel's asparagus') and trip-wires covered such possible air-landing sites as had not been flooded.

All this, the airmen knew. Just as they knew—better than most, since training flights had provided a bird's-eye view— the strength of the mighty force about to hurl itself on the enemy. From the air, southern England had come to resemble a vast arsenal. Airfields and army camps were everywhere. Between them, across downs and valleys and on flat heaths, lay great fleets of parked tanks and half-track vehicles, military lorries, jeeps and howitzers. More rested in railway yards and sidings. Round the coast, naval vessels and transports crammed natural harbours; man-made harbours, 'Mulberries', were ready to float to France.

As the gliders ghosted overhead, the biggest invasion armada ever known—more than 5,000 seacraft—had started its voyage in total blackout. That fleet would be off Normandy at first light.

Glider commander Lieutenant-Colonel Iain Murray glimpsed its dark outline from his cockpit. For the tall, leanly-handsome former Guards officer who had taken charge at home while Chatterton had been in North Africa, the flight was the culmination of hard work. This time there were to be no partly-trained pilots on a mission. The fliers were fully rehearsed in every type of landing required of them—in the mass, or for the special assaults some were briefed to make. Chatterton had put the lessons of Sicily to good effect. Now he waited at headquarters while the young colonel led the air fleet.

At dawn the seaborne assault would strike from the Cotentin Peninsula east to near Merville. The task of the airborne forces, glider men and paratroops, was to secure the flanks of the beachhead complex. American skymen were bound for the Cotentin, their target the region of St Mère-Eglise. The British objective was the eastern flank, an area between Caen and Merville traversed by the Orne and the Caen canal. Dropping by night, they would form protective shoulders for the invaders who came by day.

More air troops would land as the hours progressed. While Griffiths and Meiklejohn crossed the Channel, others in England tried to relax or sleep. Glider pilot Bob Cardy, a clerk in civilian life, was playing poker in the mess at Keevil, Wiltshire, as Griffiths had donned his battle gear. There was time for a drink with the Australian tug crew and fellow pilot Sid Longworth before turning in. Longworth, an untypically diffident Liverpudlian, was in his teens—ridiculously young, it struck Cardy, to be flying a combat glider the next day. Many already gliding to battle were mere boys.

At 2,000 ft, Griffiths was straining for a sight of France. It must be near, because he could see anti-aircraft fire directed at bombers around Caen. The weather had improved a little, the blue tug-lights of the Albemarle clearer, but the ground seemed obscured by a swirling mist. It was, in fact, smoke drifting from the guns and the bombing raid. Then it was gone and the pilots could see the snaking sheen of the Orne and the Caen canal.

'I just thought: well, this is it—the night we return to France after four years. I bawled to Jock. We both clamped our fists and feet on the controls. If one of us was hit going down, the other would be ready. I pulled the release lever. We were on our own.'

The thunder of bombers over France was familiar. To people such as Charles Le Marquand in his cottage outside Merville, Mathilde Doix of Ranville, nearer Caen, and the Gondrées of Benouville, across the Orne, the rumpus was not at first extraordinary. Monsieur Le Marquand, disturbed by the thump of guns, pulled the bedclothes higher and went to sleep again. Madame Doix awakened drowsily. Her grandson Alain, aged eleven, was shaking her.

'Wake up, grandmamma, something's happening!'

Lights were flickering on the walls, and when Alain's father, René Doix, joined them she thought it must be worse than usual—a really heavy raid. From the window, René Doix could see aircraft swooping low over the countryside.

They had an odd look. He listened carefully. Guns were firing, but the planes were making no noise. It struck him suddenly. 'My God, they're gliders, not bombing planes!'

Georges Gondrée, proprietor of a small inn near the canal bridge at Benouville, was disinclined to give up his rest. Twice his wife complained of unusual noises, and only when she persisted did he rouse himself. 'Can't you hear it?' she asked anxiously. 'Listen. It sounds like wood breaking.' Sleepily, Gondrée went to the window and opened it.

It was moonlight. From the upstairs bedroom he could see the western end of the steel bridge across the road. A German soldier was standing guard on it. The scene looked normal, though the Frenchman did hear 'snapping and crunching sounds'. Madame Gondrée joined him at the window. Alsation by birth, she spoke good German, and asked the sentry what was happening. He did not answer. To their consternation, the Gondrées realised the man was petrified.

Almost simultaneously, firing started. Collecting their two small children, the couple scuttled to the cellar where they listened to shooting outside. It was cold. The woman wore nothing but her nightdress. After a while, her husband, venturing upstairs on all-fours, looked out again. He heard talking. The words were muffled. Then he saw the shapes of soldiers by his petrol pump. Two were crouching. Between them was a dead man.

At rather less than three hours before midnight, Rommel's 15th Army had received warning that invasion was imminent. Its radio monitoring unit picked up a BBC message in code to the French underground. According to an intelligence officer, the message indicated an attack within two days. His superior, General Hans von Salmuth, was sceptical. German weather experts had ruled out the conditions for an invasion at this period. On the strength of their forecasts, and the temporary absence of General Rommel, local commanders were in relaxed mood.

Salmuth ordered the alerting of the 15th Army, occupying

the Pas de Calais, but the 7th Army in Normandy was not notified. By eleven o'clock, the general and his staff had resumed their social evening—and the first British gliders had taken off.

These formed a small group preceding Murray's main fleet. Among them were six Horsas charged with seizing adjacent bridges on the canal and the River Orne. Pilots Wallwork and Ainsworth, in the glider leading the canal drop, cast off about seven miles from Benouville, steering by compass until they saw the waterways. In the back, glider troops of the Ox. and Bucks. Light Infantry, under Major John Howard, linked arms for the impact and prayed silently.

There was little sound in the dim fuselage, just a fluttering sigh as they sped to earth. Moonlit rooftops slid across the small ports—the roofs of Ranville, where René Doix saw them pass. They were low now, expecting bullets any moment, but none came. The craft shuddered. An arrester parachute, specially fitted to slow the landing, had done its job. There was perhaps a minute to go. It seemed interminable.

Howard was by the door, prepared to throw it open at the first chance. Bren gunner Gray braced himself and kept his eyes shut. He heard Danny Brotheridge, his platoon lieutenant, say 'Here we go', then his ears were rent by a crunching roar as wheels buckled, belly grounded and, like a derailed train, they were hurtling on. In the cockpit, Ainsworth and Wallwork watched the bridge appear to race and sway towards the port wing. They had promised Howard to get close. It seemed dangerously likely they had exceeded their best hopes.

Behind them, sparks were flying from the fuselage. With the sparks came splinters, an unnerving imitation of tracer bullets, but caused in fact by friction as they ploughed through a wire fence. With a lurch, the ship halted, impelling the pilots forward. Ainsworth found himself lying in the remains of the torn fence. The iron bridge, with its tall swing mechanism, was yards away.

Men were scrambling out, stumbling on French soil, when the second and third gliders careered in to augment the force. Together, Howard's troops charged the guard-post on the near bank. 'All hell was flying. We went through some spindly trees, hurling grenades at an earthwork and blazed at the control hut against the bridge.' The Germans stood little chance. Some were asleep. The rest, dumbfounded, fired blindly, one man standing his ground to put a flare up. He fell in a storm of bullets.

The arcing flare was seen from the Orne bridge. There, pilots Pearson and Guthrie had wrestled their glider over 30-foot trees to dump its passengers as planned by the river, closely followed by a fifth plane. The sixth had landed by the Dives, the wrong river, eight miles distant. Discovering the mistake, its occupants started stealthily through the darkness towards the Orne.

Meanwhile, led by Lieutenant Brotheridge, part of Howard's force stormed over the canal to the far bank. Gray had the strap of his bren on his shoulder, firing from the hip as he went forward. Ahead, the railed pavings of the bridge fanned out towards the Gondrée establishment. Germans crouched in confusion by the small inn. Thumping on the door, one called to the inmates to open it. No one answered. Shooting wildly, the Germans backed off.

On the bridge, word had now come from the Orne contingent—'Ham and jam', the code for 'objective captured'. The signal corporal flicked the switch on his field radio. Elatedly, he signalled their own success. 'Ham and jam . . . Ham and bloody jam . . .' He kept repeating it. Others were digging in, tending casualties. Gray crossed to the petrol pump. A body lay there. A comrade joined him and they stooped to the victim. It was Brotheridge. His smock was still smouldering where an incendiary grenade had set light to it. Unseen, Georges Gondrée watched them in silent awe.

'I thought they must belong to the crew of a crashed bomber, but I was worried by the clothes they had on and by the fact that they seemed to be wearing black masks.' He was worried, too, by what might happen if he disclosed his command of English to the wrong people. Years of occupation had taught the Gondrées, like others subjected to Nazi rule, to treat strangers cautiously. More figures came from the shadows, one pointing a gun and asking in French if there were Germans in the house.

Heart thumping, Gondrée said, 'Non', and they descended suspiciously to the cellar where Madame Gondrée clasped the children. 'For a moment there was silence,' recalled the Frenchman, 'then one soldier turned to the other and said, "It's all right, chum." At last I knew they were English, and burst into tears. We all kissed them. Our faces were covered in the black paint.'

8

The Guns of Merville

Monsieur Le Marquand had heard many strange sounds in his country life, none so chilling as that which reawakened him. 'It was like an anguished creature, a beast in pain, yet no beast I could bring to mind. Then I placed the noise: a hunting horn. But what madman was hunting at dead of night?'

The madman was a British paratroop officer. His call, rending the dark coverts of Normandy, indeed struck an anguished note, for poor visibility had caused many in the sky battalions to plunge to horror, scattering others beyond recall. Plane-loads of young men had stepped into black space to sink to death off-shore, or in pathless bogs.

Those who had survived had shed their chutes and were stealing through the gloom towards the strained notes. It was a dismal start. Of the 700 men in his 9th Battalion, Lieutenant-Colonel Terence Otway found himself with 150 to pursue the task assigned to him. It was a vitally important one.

The 9th were to attack a coastal battery near Merville, a murderous threat to the sea assault. Manned by something approaching 200 soldiers, the guns were in concrete emplacements 12 ft high and 6 ft thick, buried in earth, the stronghold fenced and deeply mined on all sides. Theoretically, it was bombproof and impregnable. The plan to eliminate it—rehearsed for weeks in England on full-scale mock-ups—was complicated.

First, a hundred Lancaster bombers were to stun the defenders with heavy missiles, then Otway's 'Red Devils' would move in. Since the lightly-armed paratroopers were not equipped to tackle fortifications, a flight of gliders was to meet them with materials: mine detectors, mortars, 'Bangalore torpedoes', jeeps and light guns. Last and most hazardous stroke of the venture, three gliders with shock troops would land literally on top of the emplacement as the paratroops moved in. Already, the plan was crumbling as Otway's horns wailed.

In the patchy light, the Lancasters had mistaken Merville itself for the stronghold, and not a single bomb touched the battery. The remnants of the 9th, weaker in numbers than the garrison to be attacked, were now faced with moving against an unscathed bastion. More than ever, they needed the gliderborne equipment. But, as they waited tensely at the rendezvous, no gliders came. Above, pilots searching despairingly for the fields were frustrated by smoke from the bombing and by low cloud. Again and again they circled. The air was turbulent, the ground unreadable. They could only guess.

Of eleven Horsas loaded with crucial weapons, five eventually landed in the area, but the fields were staked with 'Rommel's asparagus' and they crashed, denying egress from their cargo holds. Five more, crossing the Channel soon after midnight, encountered the same conditions. One by one, they did their best to reach the paratroops. Only two came near. Their loads were not claimed.

Otway could no longer afford to wait. It was 02.50, and if the battery were not spiked by dawn its guns would pound the sea force. Passing the order to advance, he picked his way through a shadowy stampede of frightened bullocks towards the outer defences of the German post, his resources (as noted in battalion documents) 'Enough signals to carry on—no three inch mortars—one machine-gun—one half of one sniping party—no six-pounder guns—no jeeps or trailers or any glider stores—no sappers—no field ambulance but six medical orderlies—no mine detectors . . .'

As the depleted band reached the barbed wire and minefields, six enemy machine-guns opened up at it. Returning fire with their solitary machine-gun, the paratroops struggled to cut the wire by hand, edgily probing the mined ground with bayonets. Sweatily, on hands and knees, they searched for booby traps. At last, as ready as they could be without implements, they waited for the word to charge.

Fear and anger intermingled. Three-quarters of their comrades were lost, the bombers had missed their target, the weapons needed had not arrived. There was a final hope. The gliders due to land on the battery had yet to come.

Gliders 27, 28 and 28A lifted from Tarrant-Rushton, Dorset, an hour before midnight. Aboard the three Horsas were 58 assault troops, all volunteers, and the glider pilots. Drily, they had called the Merville mission 'the VC job,' but as a tempermental wind tossed clouds and sleet at the combinations the problems of travelling overshadowed the prospect ahead of them. Buffetted from take-off, glider 28A parted from its tug over England, forced to land by a broken rope.

In glider 28, pilots Bone and Dean tensely followed a weaving Albemarle as it attempted to avoid the worst cloud patches. The ride was rough. Despite the best efforts of the tug crew, mist engulfed them and they kept station with difficulty. About mid-Channel, stomachs lurched and with sickly certainty the sky troops sensed they were dropping towards the cold sea. The glider's arrester chute had broken open. Streaming behind, it stalled both aircraft.

With seconds to spare, Bone hit the jettison control and the chute departed. Slowly, they climbed again. The glider still flew, but the sudden drag had strained the bolts of the tail section. What might happen on landing was imponderable. The controls were sloppy, the arrester gone. Now, gunfire stabbed at them. They had reached the French coast near the Orne's mouth at little more than 1,000 ft. Dense cloud hung above as they turned for Merville.

Steadfastly, the combination circled amid gun bursts, seeking indications of the battery.

Pilots Kerr and Mickey, flying the remaining glider, had made good time to the English coast, their tug sweeping wide round Worthing, Sussex, to approach France in the same blaze of fire that had greeted Bone. This time it was accurate. Splinters flew from the fuselage and a soldier slumped badly wounded in the dim hold. Ahead, the Albemarle ploughed on. Another man cried in agony. Two more were hit as the combination joined the other in rotation above the waiting paratroops.

They were right on time, but Otway's luck had not improved. The plan called for two signals to the gliders from the land force: a mortar-fired starlight and a Rebecca-Eureka contact. The second was inoperable. Still secret, the radio device had been fitted with an explosive charge to destroy it in case of capture. This had been triggered as the parachutist with the instrument struck the ground. The star signal was impossible. Neither mortars nor starshells had reached Otway from the air drops.

Without signals, Bone and Kerr had either to return home or gamble on spotting the target as they descended. Both pilots released, watched helplessly by the crouching paratroops. Against the sky, wheeling blindly, the whispering ships looked like black bats. In turn, pursued by tracer, they passed over the battery; in turn, they veered away from it.

For Bone, every second was precious as he lost height. Searching desperately for a landmark, he was confronted by the smoke from the bombing raid. Informed of the Lancaster mission, he expected the target to be pulverised, and aimed now for the source of the emission. At 500 ft, the mistake was clear. There was time only to avoid the ruins of Merville and find a landing field. He did, saving the glider, but too far from the battery to get to it.

Kerr eased his stricken ship through the same murk, the wounded behind him in grim shape. His eye was on a dark formation on the ground where the target ought to be. Swooping, he streamed the arrester chute and prepared for impact.

Horrified, the paratroops saw the Horsa ignore the battery and crash on what its pilots had mistaken for it—an orchard, 50 yds away. Anguished officers had to restrain men from breaking cover and running to the wrecked plane. In the torn fuselage, stunned and injured passengers regained their wits in time to see not paratroops but German infantry advancing on them. They had landed in the path of a squad marching to reinforce the battery.

For Otway's band it was now or never. Again, the horn wailed. They went forward, lit garishly by German flares, lashed by machine-gun and Schmeisser fire, stooping and crawling, pausing to blaze back as they made for the concrete pits. Mines exploded. Maimed men lay amidst them, waving others to keep away. Trenches loomed. Piling in, the paratroops fought hand-to-hand with the defenders in a bedlam of screaming and grenade blasts. The horn stopped. Its owner, Lieutenant Alan Jefferson, had fallen. Lying wounded, he yelled the men on. Then, raising the horn to his lips again, he revived the unearthly notes.

At the orchard, the glider men battled to hold the reinforcing Germans off. Advancing from the matchwood of the Horsa, the crash survivors actually threw their opponents back before consolidating around the wrecked plane. They would be there, still defying the enemy, when dawn broke.

Now mayhem had gripped the battery. Otway was in the stronghold. In concrete corridors and galleries, defenders were fighting madly. The assault was fast and terrible. Hurling grenades in front of them, spraying the chambers with scorching stens, the paratroops reached the guns. One section gained a shell store. There was a shattering explosion and two men fell mangled but still alive, a third killed outright. Others were spiking guns with explosive charges.

Minutes later, a subaltern told Otway the guns were blown. Dead and crippled lay everywhere, Germans and British. Even as he reported, the subaltern clutched a mortal chest wound. His life ebbed as his comrades withdrew through the mines again. The glider troops were still holding the orchard as they pulled out.

At the same time, other glider men, wide of their objectives, were seeking friendly shadows in the Norman lanes. Scattered between the Orne and the more easterly River Dives, isolated groups of paratroopers—two or three men in many cases—were doing likewise. Occasionally, the word 'Punch' would come softly from some dark spot. A whispered 'Judy', brought relief as two groups met.

A couple of glider pilots, advancing gingerly along a road, heard a low noise. 'Punch,' breathed one, and a voice said suspiciously, *'Wer ist das?'* They dived for a ditch as Schmeisser fire drilled the lane. Too cramped to use their rifles, they managed to lob a grenade towards the enemy, then retreated frantically on hands and knees. At length, they escaped in the engulfing gloom. Encounters of a like kind were numerous.

Elsewhere, paratroops had blown four of five bridges on the Dives to prevent German crossings there. The fifth, and most important, was the target of glider missions. One of the aircraft, hit by gunfire, crashed beyond the river; another landed on the Caen side, but miles from Troarn, where the bridge stood. Unloading their jeep, the sappers in the second glider set off for the objective, raced through the sleeping town, overwhelmed the opposition and destroyed the bridge. Then, taking to the country, they returned on foot.

Seven survivors from the crashed glider swam the river and spent three days hiding and skirmishing before reaching friendly lines. By then they had marched 45 miles through the enemy, blowing up four German lorries and a staff car with hand-grenades.

Everywhere, the first dark hours of D-Day passed dramatically. Much more was to come before night ended, and some were preparing for it. Engineers parachuted near Ranville were clearing a field for the main glider landing now imminent: 68 Horsas and 4 Hamilcars of Murray's force, among the pilots Griffiths and Meiklejohn. The chosen ground had been obstructed with 'asparagus', the tall poles wired to bombs and topped with live shells. To make the job of clearance more hazardous, the toiling sappers were subjected to artillery and machine-gun fire. They were wrestling with the poles as the planes approached.

Far west, in the Contentin, hard-pressed American paratroops were waiting anxiously by the lights they had set up at Hiesville, four miles from St Mère-Eglise, to guide their own gliders to them with sorely-needed guns and jeeps. As the British skymen had jumped in the eastern area, men of the US 82nd and 101st Airborne Divisions had plumbed the night above the western peninsula, floating down over woods and forbidding swamps. Many, like their allies, had drifted from the target zones.

Some landed in St Mère-Eglise itself, plummeting on rooftops, in gardens, around the small square, where the German garrison awaited them. A bloody and brutal battle flared. Rommel's 7th Army , galvanised by the action, began to stir. As its tanks and motor columns rolled, the lightly-armed paratroops peered impatiently skywards for the glider train.

American enthusiasm for war gliders had come late. Apprised of the exploits of Air Commando with Wingate, Eisenhower had called Alison from Burma to give advice. But pilots were in short supply. In some cases, the Americans employed Wacos with a single pilot, aided by a trooper without flying skills. Brigadier-General James M. Gavin, the US airborne commander, did not envy the plight of such a man should the pilot be incapacitated over Normandy. The idea of an ordinary soldier landing a loaded glider under fire was, as Gavin put it, conducive to religious thoughts.

So, perhaps, were the stout hedges and anti-glider poles which sprouted from the gloom as the ships of the first US glider train broke through coastal flak and dipped towards French soil. Bedevilled like the jump-troops before them by tricky weather, most landed outside the planned fields.

In glider No. 1, General Pratt watched pilot Mike Murphy cast off and head for earth. A glider training commander recently from Indiana, Colonel Murphy was a noted stunt pilot. Skill could not save him from the hedgerow which loomed within seconds of touching down. The Waco crumpled. Hurled from the cockpit, Murphy lay in the hedge, both legs broken, while Pratt, crushed by the airframe, was already dead. Another airborne soldier was luckier. From the jeep in a speeding glider he saw poles rearing beside the ports, watched the wings tear like paper, and found himself incredibly safe in France. He was still sitting in the jeep. Around him, the Waco was in pieces.

On a second field, American paratroops goggled as a laden glider reduced the chimney of a farmhouse, cartwheeled across a yard and struck a stone wall. There was no sound, 'not even a moan from the wreckage'. Ship after ship landed crazily, but the Wacos were resilient. More often than not the steel-tubed structure preserved its cargo. Barely waiting for the gliders to subside, paratroops tore at the moorings of the vital guns.

9

Sky Trains

As Griff Griffiths released his Horsa and watched the blue 'glims' of the tug fade and disappear, he could see the Orne and its accompanying canal shimmering through the great skeins of smoke which blotted out much of the land below. Anti-aircraft fire had been heavy on the coast and many craft in the main train of gliders were badly hit. Three had gone down in the sea. Others had crashed on land. Of the 68 Horsas which had set out, 47 had reached the release zone, plus two of the four Hamilcars.

Gunfire continued to pound the aircraft. Griffiths felt a thump as something struck the rear of the glider, then another thump. Both he and his co-pilot, Meiklejohn, had their hands and feet on the controls, the Horsa still answering reasonably. Behind them, the medical officer they had taken aboard at the last moment was clutching the brandy bottle close to him. Apprehensively, they searched for the landmarks: the church tower, the two houses, the T of flares which should mark the landing path cleared by the parachute engineers.

It was just visible in the night, between the rooftops of Ranville and Amfreville, bordered to the west by the Sallenelles road and the River Orne.

In another Horsa, Staff-Sergeant Proctor watched a Stirling tug rage from the night ahead with all four engines on fire. Releasing from his own tug as he spotted the purple ground flares, he was forced to take evasive action by a barrage of tracer, finding himself cross-wind at 100 ft with no alternative but to land amid a forest of anti-glider poles. Yet another pilot saw a glider below him switch on its emergency lights just in time to illuminate a row of trees into which it was flying. Seconds later, the ship crashed.

Griffiths recalled his landing hazily. 'It was chaos. Flak was flying, our tail full of holes. Suddenly, the ground was coming up, the front wheel broke off and the nose went in with a crunching jolt. I saw the medical officer jump out and race away. A lot of firing was going on. We got the jeep and anti-tank gun unloaded, then paused to take stock.'

Finding the coffee flasks they had taken with them, Griffiths and Meiklejohn filled themselves with warm liquid. Their late passenger, the doctor, had left his brandy behind in his haste to leave, and they divided it between the two flasks. Half the brandy was soon gone. 'A burst of Spandau fire sent me diving to the ground, and my flask shattered. We gave some of what remained to a wounded pilot as we staunched his blood.' The man was barely recognisable, his face in a gruesome mess.

Proctor, sinking towards the anti-glider poles, cursed his own luck. Then, as the traps reared, he saw that the Germans had methodically planted them in straight lines. Manoeuvring the ship until it was flying a few feet above the poles, fuselage between the lines, he shouted to Bob Wright, his co-pilot, for full flap, thrusting the nose into the next gap. With a fierce rending of wood, the wings broke on the obstacles, the body of the glider pulling up intact.

Nearby, a Horsa of the same flight had rammed a pole nose-on. Both pilots had died horribly.

While Wright supervised the unloading of their cargo, Proctor scouted outside. The whine of bullets, aimed at him from a church tower some 500 yds distant, sent him scuttling back to the glider for a bren-gun. With this, he silenced the hostile fire, and the two pilots set out to find friends.

The crew of another Horsa, down safely, was having trouble removing the tail section to extricate the jeeps inside. After unscrewing the nuts, they could not budge it, even when one pilot jumped up and down on the section. Fear of damaging the cargo ruled out the explosive charge, and the combined tugging of pilots and jeep drivers at length exhausted everyone. For several minutes they were forced to stop and dodge paratroops tumbling from planes above. One man, a heavy bag strapped to his leg, actually landed on the tail of the glider. It held fast. The paratrooper grinned but showed no interest in their problem as he disappeared.

Encouraged by the proximity of his comrades, the glider pilots went in search of help. Somewhere, a house was burning. Passing a small orchard, they were challenged in a lane by the word 'Punch'. Answering, 'Judy', they discovered two signallers and a Canadian major who had lost their bearings. The men agreed to return to the stubborn plane. For a moment, the major looked at it, then tapped the tail tentatively. There was a creaking sigh and it fell off.

Craft were still landing. the zone littered with gliders now, many wrecked. As men strained to unship the jeeps and guns they carried, one of the great Hamilcars trundled from the gloom and, framed by shellfire, buried its nose in the dewy soil. There, exit jammed, it was hit and began to burn. Inside, the driver of the tank it carried revved grimly, released the clutch and smashed his way out through the face of the blazing pile. Gunfire criss-crossed the area, sometimes with such intensity that, as one glider pilot put it, 'it was literally raining shrapnel'.

Iain Murray, commanding the glider train, had been blessed with luck. In his Horsa the colonel carried the commander of the 6th Air Landing Brigade, Brigadier the Hon. Hugh Kindersley, and, among others, Chester Wilmot, the journalist. As Murray landed, a pole tore one of his wing-tips and a second pole was rammed by the glider's nose.

Instead of demolishing the cockpit, the obstacle collapsed harmlessly—a circumstance Murray later attributed to the deliberate engineering of some patriotic Frenchman pressed to work for the enemy.

Apart from Wilmot's tape-recorder, which had been smashed by a fragment of German shell, the colonel's charges arrived intact. The fire they encountered was spasmodic, and, making their way to the glider pilot rendezvous, they waited for others to join them there.

Soon, as dawn rose, seaborne forces would fight their way ashore to the west, spreading into the country beyond the Orne and the canal, their flank linking with the airborne men at the crossings secured by the glider troops. To the north of Murray's group, the shattered Merville battery would be silent as the ships approached. To the east, German forces advancing to the Dives would find its bridges in rubble on the water bed. From confusion, shape was forming—but still the night was disordered by roaming bands from both sides, none sure where they would encounter the enemy.

Griffiths and Meiklejohn, having left their anti-tank team, set off for the rendezvous by dark hedgerows in which growing numbers of shadowy figures were bent on their own missions. Squads of paratroops and Commandos, black-faced, armed to the teeth, exchanged cursory words before vanishing as abruptly as they appeared.

Elsewhere, Proctor and Wright, having run into heavy fire, decided on a detour which brought them, after a mile or so, to a village street. The place seemed completely deserted. Picking their way cautiously through spookily silent dwellings, they emerged at a road junction to hear the crunch of a tracked vehicle approaching them. In the half-light, they could see it was full of troops. 'Germans,' muttered Proctor.

Crouching in a ditch, the glider pilots took out a grenade apiece and removed the pins. As the vehicle drew abreast of them it stopped and Proctor was on the point of hurling his grenade when a voice said: 'I say, you chaps, can you tell me the name of this village?'

The machine was a bren-carrier, and the captain in charge, having explained that he was scouting for elements of a Panzer unit believed to be nearby, ordered his driver forward. The two pilots were alone again, searching anxiously for the discarded pins of the grenades they clutched. It was almost light before, lost and weary, they stumbled on a slit-trench by an orchard, and someone asked: 'Where the hell have you been?'

Meanwhile, the pilots who had lost time over the jammed tail had unloaded the glider and started for the rendezvous when a Horsa swooped over them and landed not far away. Joining up with its crew, they headed into the bewildering and edgy gloom. At one point they were pinned down by automatic fire before, escaping through some trees, they came on a country house where a middle-aged Frenchwoman was preparing to take a drink to a wounded soldier. The neighbouring house, she told them, was a German base, occupied by about 75 men. Intent on reporting the fact, the pilots were narrowly missed by sniper fire as they approached divisional headquarters, which they had located in a farm building.

At dawn the ground trembled. Allied planes were pattern-bombing the beaches as a prelude to the sea landings. Several miles inland, repercussions shook the fox-holes in which many of the pilots were now entrenched around headquarters and the glider zone. Their numbers suggested fewer losses than some had feared. In fact, one British glider in five had been lost, 42 pilots killed and 9 wounded out of 144 in the night action. It was a lot, but the achievement had been great, and there was more ahead.

The largest glider operation of D-Day in the British sector, by daylight, was yet to come. Two hundred and fifty gliders were due with 7,500 men of the 6th Airlanding Brigade, and, as German pressure mounted against the tiring night squads, reinforcements were looked for with anxious and bleary eyes. By afternoon, pilots on the ground were taking benzedrene tablets to stay alert.

Into evening, the German gun and mortar fire intensified. Among the glider men dug in round the landing zones it was evident the perimeter was hard pressed, the hour critical. Then, as one reported it, 'above the noise of the firing we heard the approach of many aircraft, the engines became a roar, and the firing seemed to stop. Even the Germans were struck dumb by what they saw: a magnificent sight, the air full of gliders sweeping in towards the German lines, turning lazily, making a left-hand circuit overhead . . .'

Part of the force was making for the original landing area, part for a new one just west of the Caen canal. The silence was short-lived. Suddenly, 'an absolute inferno of noise broke out', and the land was plastered with missiles as the Germans sought the range of the landing fields. Heads-down in their holes, the waiting pilots heard the whistle of Horsas as their comrades swept in.

The greatest glider fleet yet launched had climbed from the breast of southern England on a glorious June evening, the sinking sun blazing through refulgent cloud strands as the combinations streamed for France. Glider pilot Bob Cardy could see the aerial rendezvous, Bognor Regis, below the shimmering bulk of the Stirling tug. The lift-off from Keevil, in Wiltshire, had been smooth. Now, after months of rehearsals, weeks of studying air photos, testing cargo weights, it was on—the sky dotted with wooden chariots.

Ahead, he could make out the Stirling gunner, watchful in the sunlight that bathed his perspex turret. Never had such a fowler's feast been presented to the Luftwaffe. For the hour and 50 minutes they would be aloft, the lives of 8,000 glider troops and pilots were in the hands of their fighter escort: the silver shoal glimpsed through the roof of the cabin, then lost to sight. It was a far cry, thought Cardy, from the clerk's desk he once occupied.

Beside him, 19-year-old Sergeant Sid Longworth surveyed the blaze of light which marked the naval barrage off the French coast. From the air, the sight was awesome.

Nothing, it seemed to Cardy, could survive such massive punishment.

Glider pilot Leslie Foster watched it from a cockpit enhanced by pin-up pictures of shapely girls. Approaching the French coast at 1,500 ft, he had taken over the controls from his fellow staff-sergeant, Tom Pearce. 'We could see the vast force of ships pouring shells and rockets into the defences of the Germans. Smoke rose into the sky as the missiles landed, and through the haze a British plane dived down in flames. The scene was both exciting and terrifying, magnificent yet appalling.'

Unmolested, the great train of tugs and gliders streamed on. In another Horsa, the troops had broken open their survival rations and were munching barley sugar. Looking forward into the cockpit, Major Wheldon saw sweat running down the back of the pilot's neck as they crossed the coast. It ran in two trickles, 'like bacon fat', he observed. Turning to the burdened hold, he was amazed to find his company runner, Mullins, fast asleep. 'Come on, Mullins,' chided Wheldon, 'we're invading Europe.'

The ship was shuddering. To the troops in the fuselage it was like being 'in a very old railway carriage yanked across the sky', a rough ride they knew would smoothen with mouth-drying abruptness as they released and descended to the battlefield. The descent was the time that they most feared. 'Casting off now,' the pilot said.

Cardy, spotting the church tower landmark, passed the same word. In his earphones, an Australian voice from the tug responded, 'Buy you a pint when you get back'.

Foster's tug captain was Canadian. 'OK, matchbox,' he drawled as they cast off. 'The best of luck.'

Still no Luftwaffe, and little flak. It had been peaceful—too peaceful, it seemed to Pearce, 'like an exercise'. But now, as they went down turning steadily on full flap, the air was suddenly crowded with obstacles: other gliders, discarded towropes, parachutes, The smiling girlie pictures had lost relevance. Eyes were on the ground, the wrecked planes from the night drop, brown mushrooms which sprouted as mortar bombs burst.

Suddenly, Pearce was shouting and Foster, alerted, saw a Horsa loom sharply beneath their own ship. Yanking back the stick, he was aware of 'a terrible tearing, crashing sound' and, watching the other craft hang under them a moment, saw it fall away, his wheels with it. On the verge of stalling, Foster hauled up his flaps and put the nose down. The speed increased.

Cardy, on a straight approach from 1,000 ft, was descending swiftly when he noticed that many gliders on the landing zone had their wings off. Veering, he aimed for an adjacent field which seemed free of poles. It was a safe landing, but the back would not release to let out the jeep and trailers he was carrying. Grabbing a saw they carried he clambered on top of the fuselage and, with Longworth, tore savagely at the wooden frame as shots flew over them.

The Hamilcar in which tank commander Major Barnett was travelling did not avoid the poles. As the huge ship ploughed down at 80 mph, Tetrarch tank in its bowels already revving, half a wing was dragged off by a post and the crippled giant lurched to a juddering halt. Discarding moorings, the tank crew slammed hatches and, accelerating, crunched out through the open nose. Another Hamilcar smashed into an unloaded Tetrarch, bowling it over like a toy tank.

Above the drub of automatic fire and crump of mortars, the whistle of gliders was now constant as they landed. Almost in slow motion, a Horsa rose on its snout and sank back again. Men burst from it, crouched low, then ran for a nearby wood.

Foster, extricating his plane from the air collision, kept the nose down. There was no sound from the troops in the back, just the roaring of the slipstream as speed increased. At 110 mph, he rammed on the flaps and pulled the nose up. He was coming into a cornfield with trees at the far end. Without wheels, he could not brake the ship. 'We were tearing through the high French corn, red earth pouring through a broken door—nothing but the long straight parting of the corn, and then, suddenly, an open patch before the trees.'

He kicked hard on the rudder bar. Spuming soil, the glider slewed through a half-circle, just missed the trees, and capsized as the port wing fell off the plane. Hacking an escape from the wreckage, crew and passengers found, to their astonishment, that none was harmed. Not far away lay the Horsa which had hit them. They could do nothing for the occupants. Losing its tail in the crash, it had plunged vertically from 600 ft.

Everywhere, glider men were heading for action—in jeeps, on foot, in tanks, with vital guns. Taking cover with one of his company, an officer of the Royal Ulster Rifles saw a mystical glaze in the man's eyes. 'Sorr,' crooned the rifleman in devout tones, ' 'tis a miracle. Not one casualty. Not a single bloody man. Every bloody man's arrived unharmed. The whole bloody company's here. 'Tis a bloody miracle.' It was almost dusk, and in the soft summer gloaming the thanksgiving came near to summarizing the operation. One tug had crashed, one had ditched. Less than five per cent of the gliders had come to grief.

Through the night, the newly-arrived glider pilots bolstered their weary comrades in defence around the landing zones. Together with the paratroops, the men they had lifted were to hold the left flank of the invasion for more than two months, until the Allied build-up was complete and the break-out started. Meanwhile, under orders to return to their bases at the first chance, the pilots made for the beaches next morning in cautious groups.

The roads were chaotic, filled with incoming seaborne forces, imperilled by snipers and pockets of German infantry. It had taken Cardy and Longworth an hour to saw the tail off their Horsa and release its load, but neither they nor their passengers had been hit. Now they made for the shore with cocked tommy-guns. 'Young fellows were wading in as we were going home again. It hardly seemed reasonable; hardly possible it had happened. Within hours we were in England, had showered and were boozing in a wayside pub.'

Like most of the pilots, he reached land at Newhaven, the Sussex port. It was low tide when Griffiths landed and he had to climb a long steel ladder beside the quay. Rusty and slippery with seaweed, it seemed interminable. He had not slept for two days and nights, and each rung sapped his dwindling strength. 'I just made it, but hanging on at that height scared the life from me.'

1 A crashed German glider which came to grief in the disastrous Crete
   operation of 6 June 1941 (IWM)

2 Early days: Hotspur gliders in training at the RAF Glider Training
   School (Fox)

3 A 1941 Hotspur built by Slingsby (IWM)

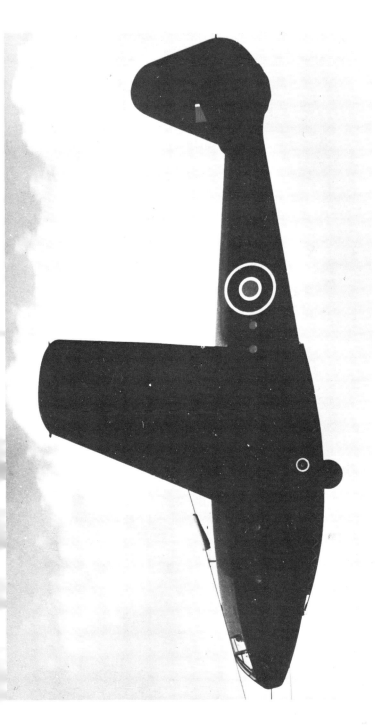

4 A Slingsby Hengist glider which could seat 15 troops. Only 14 gliders of this model were built (IWM)

5　Prototype of the famous Horsa built at Christchurch, Hants. (IWM)

6　A Horsa on an early training flight (IWM)

7　*An early model of the Hadrian on a test flight (IWM)*

8　*A Hamilcar, built primarily for transporting heavy equipment, disgorges a tank (IWM)*

9 *Glider pilots in training, under instruction (IWM)*

10 *Horsa gliders coming in to land on a training flight 'somewhere in Britain' (IWM)*

11 *Horsas in training being towed by Whitley bombers (Planet News)*

12 *A jeep, trailer and motorcyclist leaving their glider after a training flight (IWM)*

13 A 'sea' of Horsas at the RAF Transport Command Training Station at Netheravon (IWM)

14 Horsas being stockpiled 'somewhere in England' (IWM)

15 *Airborne troops synchronizing watches before taking off for the invasion of France (IWM)*

16 *Dawn on D-Day: a glider takes off (IWM)*

17 The air armada on its way to France (IWM)

18 Pegasus Bridge, showing how close the coup de main *party, led by
Major John Howard, landed (IWM)*

19 *The glider landing zone at Pegasus Bridge (IWM)*

20 *Hamilcar gliders landing in Normandy on 6 June 1944 (IWM)*

21 This glider's unhappy landing reveals the wing construction (IWM)

22 *Gliderborne troops who perished in the initial landing on 6 June 1944 at Hiesville, Normandy (Robert Hunt Library)*

23 *A member of an American airborne unit lies dead in the wreckage of his glider near Carentan, June 1944 (Robert Hunt Library)*

24 A 6th Divisional landing zone in Normandy (IWM)

Part Two

From Rhine to Rhine

10

Market Forces

The success of Normandy greatly strengthened the glider lobby led by Chatterton and already supported by Browning and the RAF's 'fairy godmother of the Cinderella service', as Wright called him, Air Vice Marshal Leslie Hollinghurst. In August 1944, Eisenhower set up a combined command, the First Allied Airborne Army, under Lieutenant General Lewis H. Brereton, an American veteran, with Browning as his deputy.

Brereton was an old advocate of landing troops in aircraft. In the First World War he had suggested just such a plan as a means of overcoming the trench war deadlock. It had not met with much enthusiasm. Now, he was backed by zealots. But their patience was being strained. Again and again since the Normandy landings, glider crews had been alerted for further actions, none of which had got off the ground. Pilots had been briefed and re-briefed. Gliders had been loaded, tugs fuelled. Each time, the scheme was cancelled for some reason.

There was 'Axehead', a plan to capture Seine bridges; 'Linnet', a projected landing inside Belgium; 'Linnet II', to close the Maastricht gap behind the enemy; 'Infatuate', a proposed assault on Walcheren; and so on. By September, 16 schemes had been aborted in three months, some discarded as impractical, more terminated by the sheer speed of an Allied advance which often surprised its own planners as much as the Germans.

In mid-September, glider and tug pilots at stations across eastern and southern England trudged to the briefing huts with some scepticism to hear—was it the eighteenth or nineteenth scheme? At least the scale of 'Market' was novel: almost every British glider pilot available was involved, together with an unprecedented number of Americans. It was, they were promised, 'the big one'.

Back in the billets, the usual collection of ammunition and ration boxes began to pile up on beds, Piats and brens to fill the floor space. Grenades were primed and rifles cleaned. On the fields, long lines of anti-tank guns and 75 mm howitzers were hauled to the maws of the gliders and lashed down. By late evening before the morning of lift-off doubts diminished and some pilots, like Gordon Jenks, began to wish they had consumed rather less beer.

Staff-Sergeant Jenks awoke with a thick head and a strong suspicion, as he told his second pilot, that 'They're not kidding this time—we're really going'. After a wash and shave, he stuck his head under a cold water tap for two minutes and felt better. Dressing, he picked up his flying helmet and went for coffee, the only substance his stomach would tolerate.

Other pilots did not bother to shave for the flight ahead. At Fairford, Gloucestershire, those who did found the hush in the wash house unusual. It was chill and still dark outside. Staff-Sergeant Miller, a survivor of Sicily, removed his beard by the light of a dim bulb, peering in a fragment of broken mirror he had carried for months, a soldier's talisman. Breakfast convinced him the flight was on. There were two eggs with the bacon, the tea was exceptionally strong and sweet, the WAAFs smiled 'in a sad sort of way' at the glider men.

At Keevil, Bob Cardy was so strongly of the same opinion

that he emptied his pockets of his valuables, including a gold cigarette case and £40 he had won at poker the night before, and pressed them spontaneously in the hands of a WAAF called Paddy, asking her to mind them for him. She put them in her pocket and said she would.

Twelve days earlier, Eisenhower had ordered Brereton to support Montgomery's 21st Army Group in its objective of reaching and crossing the River Rhine. The Germans, after a long retreat from the Seine, were fighting defensively south of Holland, between Antwerp and Maastricht, the line held fiercely by what remained of some good divisions but backed by few reserves and depleted in armoured strength. Montgomery, not enamoured of Eisenhower's doctrine of broad attack, favoured a bold northward thrust through Holland on a narrow front before turning east to the Ruhr and Berlin. For this, he needed Brereton's airborne army to secure a number of river crossings ahead of the main force.

The line of advance selected to the Rhine was Eindhoven, Grave, Nijmegen and Arnhem, the last on the Rhine itself, rather less than 70 miles behind the German front. Other notable streams to be traversed were the Maas at Grave and the Waal at Nijmegen, a few miles away. The plan was for the simultaneous seizure of the three regions—Eindhoven, Grave-Nijmegen and Arnhem—by airborne forces, while the British Second Army thrust forward on this axis along what was termed somewhat loosely 'an Airborne carpet'.

The ground operation was coded 'Garden', the whole offensive transmitted to Dutch Resistance, then under strong pressure from the SS, as 'Market Garden'. According to intelligence, there was a German armoured corps northeast of Arnhem, but it was refitting, thus immobilized. Arnhem itself was believed not to be strongly garrisoned.

Spearheading the Second Army in its ground advance would be the Guards Armoured Division of 30 Corps. The timetable called for it to reach Eindhoven within eight hours of Zero-hour, Nijmegen by noon the second day and

Arnhem by noon the third day. While the air landings at Eindhoven and Nijmegen would serve to expedite the ground thrust, the landing at Arnhem itself would not only hold the bridge open for the offensive but deny it to countering forces.

In principle the scheme was simple. Three airborne divisions would land, one in each region. Eindhoven would be covered by the 101st American Airborne Division; Nijmegen by the 82nd American; Arnhem by the 1st British Airborne Division. The Americans would provide the aircraft for all the main parachute drops; the RAF (38 and 46 Groups) for the glider-towing, pathfinder dropping and re-supply at Arnhem. A British Airborne Corps HQ would be transported to Nijmegen by gliders and tugs of the British force.

In detail, there were problems. Arnhem, the region deepest into enemy territory, raised difficulties for the planners concerning landing zones. The ground to the south of the river was low-lying polderland, reclaimed country webbed with countless dykes and flood banks. With poor roads, little cover and dominated by such guns as might be mounted on the higher ground north of the river, it was risky terrain for air landing. On the other hand, it offered the closest possibility to the city and the bridge there.

As an alternative, a region north of the river and west of Arnhem contained inviting grassy clearings with good wooded cover for assembly, but meant that landings would be up to eight miles from the objective. Both Chatterton and the RAF favoured this territory, agreeing that the polder was unsuitable for mass landings. Final word was with the commander of 1st Airborne.

Major General Robert 'Roy' Urquhart was new to the sky force, chosen as a tough, bold commander with thoughtful qualities. His dilemma was not enviable. Depending to a large degree on the evidence of flying men, he was constrained to choose between the possibilities of fighting several miles towards his objective from the safer landing area, or of risking heavy landing losses to reduce the ground distance to the bridge. After a fortnight of discussion between the services, the RAF's Lawrence Wright called on Urquhart. He found the broad, bear-like figure of the general in a garden at Moor Park, north of London, pouring over an easel which held the battle plan.

More than 680 gliders were to be flown by the British force, in day formations—a larger number by the Americans. It was a massive air operation, and, for want of more tugs, the Arnhem lift was phased over two days, with re-supply on the third day. As a consequence, Urquhart was faced with an initial task not only of seizing the bridge, but of deploying a substantial portion of his force in defence of the landing grounds and communications until the later landings had been made. It was a strong argument against the more distant landing zone.

'We shall be too thin on the ground,' the general predicted, as Wright recalled it. The commander then 're-opened the question of landing gliders on the polder, making me restate the pros and cons of the terrain'. From an airman's viewpoint there were few pros. Apart from the banks and ditches, the only possible fields were flanked by power cables and near a battery of 12 anti-aircraft guns. A formidable dyke enclosed this area. Reluctantly, Urquhart decided on the north bank.

Flight plans were now made. The bases for the operation were dispersed in two broad areas: a southern group of eight British and six US airfields stretching west from Boreham and Chipping Ongar in Essex to Keevil and Tarrant Rushton in Wiltshire and Dorset, and an eastern group of eight US airfields around Grantham, Lincolnshire. Two air routes were planned. Duplication was necessary because of the length of the column—so great, had only one route been allowed, that the Germans might have time on the first day to organise attacks on the rear elements. On the following days, a route option could prove useful should weather or enemy action become troublesome.

The northern route, crossing Aldeburgh on the Suffolk

coast and Schouwen Island, involved a flight of about 80 miles over enemy-occupied Dutch territory. The southern route crossed by North Foreland, Kent, to Belgium, veering north behind Allied lines at Gheel, east of Antwerp. The distance over enemy territory by this route was between 60 and 70 miles. It was to be used by the US 101st Division, while the British 1st and US 82nd took the northern route.

The combinations were to fly in three parallel streams, giving a column time-length on the first day of about 65 minutes. Radio and visual beacons were arranged as guides on the English coast, on a ship in the North Sea, and at the Gheel turning point. Paratroop pathfinder teams would land ahead of the gliders to mark the landing fields with coloured panels and smoke. They would also operate Eureka beacons.

No effort was spared to organise protection for the air fleets. All known German anti-aircraft batteries on the routes were to be attacked by the 8th USAAF and the RAF. More than 800 B-17 bombers and some 370 Typhoon and other fighter-bombers would blast the enemy guns with 3,000 tons of bombs, and cannon fire, on the first day. Throughout the lifts, American fighters would provide cover against air attack, while British bombers hit enemy fighter fields. Forty aircraft were to drop dummy parachutists west of Utrecht as a feint. Elsewhere, a general effort was planned to distract German attention by air activity.

The day chosen for the first flights was 17 September, a Sunday. Take-off was to be under way by ten o'clock that morning; landings in full operation some two hours and 40 minutes later. Weather forecasts, as the time approached, were for a promising five-day period, with acceptable cloud bases—an important factor, since blind-flying was ruled out by the density of the formations which would take the air.

Since virtually the whole of Britain's glider pilot strength would be in operation, there was a vital requirement to withdraw the fliers as swiftly as possible once landed and, until this was done, to avoid costly casualties to the pilot force in ground battles. With limited exceptions, glider pilots were to be deployed, after landing, in defensive roles. Until they returned, there would be no reserves.

Speed was crucial to the whole plan. The safety of each airborne force depended on the swift success of the others and the rapid advance of the armoured thrust of the Second Army. Of none was this truer than the Arnhem contingent, especially vulnerable in the event of a hold-up at Eindhoven or Nijmegen. A single lightly-armed division deep in enemy territory could expect to survive very few days—a fact acknowledged by the three-day schedule of the relieving corps.

Staff-Sergeant Jenks checked the controls of his Hamilcar. Below in the great hold were a 17-pounder anti-tank gun and trailer, eight men, a 3-ton lorry and a supply of high explosive shells. Making himself as comfortable as possible, he pulled his safety-belt tight and fastened it. All round were tugs and gliders: Halifaxes, Horsas, Hamilcars. The combination in front began to move. The tow-master signalled. It was Jenks's turn. Inscribed in large chalked letters on the glider were the words 'Bun House'—the name of his local pub.

At Great Dunmow, Essex, Derrick Shingleton, a fair-complexioned young man, tall and powerful, fixed his strappings beside co-pilot Raymond Percival. Some time earlier, Shingleton's pretty WAAF girl friend, Celia, had agreed to marry him. It would be, he told himself, the first thing he arranged when he got back.

At Broadwell, near Brize Norton, Lieutenant-Colonel John Place's Horsa began to roll. The weather was moderately bright but overcast. On board were 28 men of the Border Regiment, their platoon equipment, and co-pilot Ralph Maltby, the wing intelligence officer. Place noted that his watch gave precisely 09.45.

Wherever they took off, the rest of the aerodrome turned out to watch. Among the bystanders were glider pilots due to fly the second day—men such as Staff-Sergeant George Betts at Keevil, one of the older pilots, 'Ricky' Rickword his co-pilot, and Leslie Gibbons of D Squadron, who had promised to meet his mates at Arnhem next morning.

Miller pulled the steps of his Horsa inside, double-checked the door lock and joined his fellow pilot, Tom Hollingsworth, in the cockpit. One of the soldiers in the fuselage, he noticed, was eating an apple and reading a Sunday paper. The cockpit was stuffy. Through the perspex, he watched the ground crew plug the towline into the glider's wings and the tail of the Stirling tug. As the Horsa began to move, he glimpsed a line of airmen and WAAFs waving. He waved back. His lips were dry. He tried to lick them but his tongue was in the same state.

I I

Day Flight, Holland

At 3,000 ft, Miller felt easier. Ahead, the stream of tugs and gliders seemed motionless, a slow rise and fall their only movement. The air was calm. From time to time, over the North Sea, the waves reflected a bright sparkle, or were frothed by a rescue launch. Rummaging in the cockpit, Miller came up with a large army thermos flask and handed Hollingsworth a cup of tea. The pilot sipped it, flying with one hand. Miller sat back.

There was a chummy sameness about the gliders. Drab and prosaic, they offered few concessions to rank or style. In one, General Urquhart, flown by Murray, commander of the Ranville train, was being yanked to battle on a rope's end. In another, General Browning, bound for Nijmegen with corps headquarters, perched on an upturned beer crate behind his pilot, Chatterton. In the 'Bun House', Jenks's passengers shuddered as the big ship hit the slipstream of the tug. For a moment, before evading the turbulence, Jenks held them there for the hell of it.

Moving into the fuselage of his Horsa, Miller found an apparently cheerful crew, save for one man who was airsick. As the glider pilot returned to the cockpit, something flashed alongside, and he watched a Typhoon race ahead towards the

Dutch coast. Two more of the fighters passed his wingtip, one of the pilots waving before banking and speeding on. Looking upwards, Miller saw a huge formation of fighters cruising a few thousand feet above the gliders.

Elated suddenly, he grinned at Hollingsworth, shouting an account of what he could see to the others through the cabin door.

It had been a good start. Of 320 gliders for Arnhem on the first day, only one failed to get off. Another returned to base, its tug in trouble, but both were reflighted with the second lift. So were most of a further 24 ships which had come adrift before the English coast in squabs of low cloud. Four more ditched in the North Sea, one shelled by a German coastal battery. All the crews were picked up. Ahead, the sweeping fighters reported few hostile aircraft, these routed by Allied squadrons.

Miller saw the black line of the Dutch coast clearly etched between the sea and the flooding the Germans had contrived against invasion. Further inland, the sludge of mud and water turned to green fields, flat farmlands spreading away into a distant haze. Below, churches were emptying, lanes and canal paths occupied by groups of people gazing up at the armada—an army soon to be descending so densely that, as the German reporter Erwin Kirchoff put it, it would look 'as if the down-coming masses would suffocate all life on earth'.

Fascinated, Miller and Hollingsworth picked out the village of Steenbergen and, on the road from it, the white and black striped poles of a German road block, a car stopped by it.

Chatterton, bound for Nijmegen with the airborne staffs, was overtaken by scurrying Spitfires as he followed his Stirling tug. The cabin was bright with sunshine, and Browning, from his beer crate behind the pilots, relayed a commentary to subordinates in the darker fuselage. The mood was buoyant when they reached the release zone and cast off. Banking, Chatterton trimmed the craft, selected a small allotment garden near some cottages, and landed in the cabbage patch.

The scene was extraordinarily calm. 'A few old Dutch peasants came and looked at us.' Browning was standing near the glider in immaculate barathea, trousers knife-edged, holster gleaming. He wore one kid glove, carrying the other and a swagger cane. There was no indication of armed action. It struck Chatterton as strange and rather eerie—not quite right.

John Place found his first sight of Holland depressing. On the way out, his tug pilot, Wing-Commander 'Jeff' Jefferson, had informed him that his aircraft lacked power, and they had decided to omit a dog-leg on the route, rejoining the stream at the Dutch coast. Here, Place and co-pilot Ralph Maltby were puzzled by a wavy white streak which shot up from the ground, curving high above them in the bright sky. They had watched a V2 rocket launched at England.

Here and there a roof, a few trees, rose from the floods, or a cluster of roofs and a church steeple showed where a village was half submerged. They saw no life below.

Jenks was watching fighters dive on German guns. Wherever an anti-aircraft battery opened up, the rocket-firing Typhoons homed in on it. Nevertheless, a few puffs of white smoke were appearing around the 'Bun House', and the pilot felt the bumps from them. There had been some teasing between pilots and the artillerymen in the hold. Now, the voice which shouted up had an earnest ring. 'The bloody glider's on fire!' it informed Jenks.

Smoke was coming from the port wing, near the fuselage, where a piece of hot shrapnel was smouldering. Another lump had entered the hold, hit a gunner on the hand, dropped to the glider's floor. It filled the crammed cavern with fumes, but had not disabled the Hamilcar. The 'Bun House' held course. At the same time, Jenks noticed that his air-speed and altimeter dials had packed up.

Arnhem was drawing near. Southwest, near S'Hertongenbosch, Miller saw shellfire near his own ship. The glider shook, shrapnel striking the fuselage with a rapid drubbing, like the sound of a woodpecker, Miller thought. 'I hunched and tensed myself.' Then it was gone. Miller was sweating. Hollingsworth, flying the aircraft, looked distinctly pale.

Wing-Commander Jefferson had hauled his combination back on stream. About 30 minutes short of Arnhem, Place, following, was appalled to hear a shout from his infantry passengers: 'Sir, sir, the tail's coming off!' For a couple of seconds, he met Maltby's gaze in silence, then, very gingerly, tested elevators and rudder by pitching and yawing the glider. It seemed all right. Maltby scrambling astern to investigate, returned looking happier. So far as could be seen, nothing was wrong. He thought the men had been frightened by flak explosions.

Maltby now flew while Place consulted his map to check their progress. Almost immediately, he heard a strange swishing sound and saw red sparks shooting upwards by the port window. Suddenly, there was a tremendous bang in the cockpit, a reek of cordite, and Maltby rolled sideways in his straps, limp. Place had grabbed the control column. Bawling for help, he told the platoon sergeant who came forward to see what he could do for the co-pilot. Maltby was dead. Tersely, Place ordered the sergeant to leave him, and shut the door.

Stunned and 'considerably frightened', the colonel realized that if he was hit there was nobody aboard who could fly the craft. Telling Jefferson the position, he asked the tug pilot to 'weave a bit'. Jefferson, already nursing his plane, replied that he did not have enough boost.

Miller was feeling the tension now. The tug ahead had began to roll and wallow, as if weary of the long strain. Below to starboard, he could see the main Eindhoven-Arnhem road. His brow was moist as he handed over to Hollingsworth, spreading his own map. Ewijk, Valburg, Lienden—the points he had marked fell away behind. Looking up from the ground and map, he saw tugs diving and wheeling, gliders flying free. Below was the Rhine. 'It looked incredibly tranquil, as rivers do.'

Arnhem graced the north bank. It had great dignity: tall houses, tree-lined avenues, palatial fifteenth-century town hall, the old churches of St Walburgis and St Eusebius. From the road bridge, the river snaked west in a series of broad curves, the first reaching its most northerly point at St Elizabeth's Hospital, near the edge of the city; the second, towards the fine wooded suburb of Oosterbeek. Where the next curve ran north, the pilots could see three villages ranged northeast in park and farmland—Renkum, Heelsum and Wolfheze.

Round Heelsum and Wolfheze, five or six miles west of Arnhem, were the main glider landing zones. Miller was looking for a triangular-shaped wood, a farm at one corner. The region was quilted with fields and forests.

Other pilots searched for their own zones. Shingleton and Percival landed east of Wolfheze, northwest of Oosterbeek. As their Horsa touched down, a shot-up tail section failed to respond to the controls, the ship swung violently sideways and broke in two. Remarkably, no one was badly hurt. The crew performed the swiftest unloading of a jeep and gun that Shingleton had ever seen.

Miller spotted his farmhouse, somehow dodged a glider which swung across his approach, and pinched into the field over towering trees. Dust billowed. Losing steerage at about 20 mph, he dropped the controls, tearing at his harness release pins. Behind, he heard the sound of doors opening, and a blast of cool air swept the cabin. He had one thought: to get out before another glider dropped on top of them, or they were raked by German gunfire.

Jenks saw his landing field near a railway embankment. The Hamilcars ahead had cast off. Thanking his tug captain for the ride, he released the 'Bun House' and took stock. 'The sky was chaotic. Worse than Piccadilly Circus in the rush hour.' Without instruments to tell him his height and speed, he decided to get on the tail of the glider in front and go down with it. Beneath the port wing he saw another Hamilcar travelling low and fast. It hit the railway embankment, somersaulting with a vivid flash. 'I wondered which of my pals was in that one.'

Beyond the embankment, he could see a third Hamilcar landing. It was careering wildly, breaking up. Telling his second-pilot to watch for other gliders, Jenks concentrated on the ship ahead. It touched down at speed. The ground must have been very soft, he thought, because 'the Hamilcar promptly dug its wheels in and flipped over on its back'. There was another flash as the heavy cargo crashed down on the hapless crew.

Determined to avoid the field, Jenks lowered his nose to gain impulse, levelled out a few feet from the ground and coaxed the mammoth over the far fence. It touched down perfectly, trundled 30 or 40 yds, then obeyed the brakes.

Place parted from his tug with a dead co-pilot and most of his flying panel shattered. To reduce the chance of being hit himself, dooming his passengers, he had resolved to make a steep approach. For this he would need flaps, and he was concerned lest the air bottles operating them had been smashed. As the towline snaked away, he tried the air-brake lever. The flaps worked. 'I went straight down,' he recalled, 'almost vertically.'

At the conclusion of his landing a shaken platoon de-bussed, sprawling defensively on the ground. Two of the men had been wounded in the air. They were tended, the dead pilot carried beneath a wing. A young private approached Place as he moved off. 'Sir, I just want to thank you,' the boy said.

Another glider pilot, Major Ian Toler, had watched a paratroop-carrying Dakota catch fire as he crossed Holland. Thankfully, he saw the troops bale out, followed by the crew, before the plane dived. With more speed than he wanted, Toler overshot his boundary on landing but was pulled up by the soft ground. Leaping from the glider, he lay panting beside Staff-Sergeant Shackleton, his second-pilot, sten at readiness. So anxious were their South Staffordshire passengers that they drove their jeep from the Horsa without a ramp, the vehicle falling with a mighty bounce.

More Staffordshires, flown by glider pilot Brandon Geary, had strapped themselves tightly to their seats approaching Arnhem. Geary made a diving descent. It seemed to Major Cain, who was a passenger, that they were at treetop height when they levelled off. With a flourish, Geary dumped them in a ploughed field. It was fine country, neatly husbanded, thick with great elms. The only firing, it seemed to Cain, was far away.

Some were less fortunate. Two pilots landed in the sights of a German patrol whose machine-gunner wounded both fliers, and several passengers, before hastily shifting from the area. Nor had all the gliders reached Arnhem. Nine fell in Holland on the way, some with broken ropes. Lieutenant Turrell and his co-pilot were forced down by ground fire south of the Rhine where a band of Dutchmen helped to unload the plane. Guided by their new friends, including the local priest, they headed north, soon disarming six Germans whom they locked in a police cell. The glidermen reached the division after ferrying the river at a quiet spot.

Cardy had landed accurately, shaken only by fouling a shallow dyke. It was quiet—a lot quieter, he reflected, than Normandy. Warned that some of the Dutch might be pro-German, he was agreeably surprised when the owner of the first house he reached with Longworth came out and greeted them in English. 'I have a friend,' exclaimed the man, 'who lived in England. Perhaps you would like a word with him on the telephone. He lives across the Rhine.'

Loath to disappoint, Cardy followed the Dutchman indoors. 'It seemed ludicrous, but there I was, barely landed in hostile country, exchanging trivial generalities about British life with someone I'd never met and could not see. I talked for a while and put the phone down.' Contented, the householder wished the pilots good-day and they moved on.

Others stopped to watch as a roar of engines announced Dakotas bearing paratroops. They came in at 500 ft, men tumbling in scores through their slipstreams until the air was thick with multicoloured parachutes. Within minutes the skymen were trailing off past the gliderborne guns, leaving ground and trees littered with brilliant silks.

Urquhart, landed nearby by Murray, was impressed with them. Watching his men group in the parklands, he felt proud of their skills and purposefulness. That so many—most of the glider troops—would be required to guard the landing zones was regrettable, but the force was intact, the paratroops starting for the bridge immediately. The landing had gone well. Some specially armed reconnaissance jeeps had been lost with the 38 gliders which had not arrived. For the rest, predictions that the area was sound had been justified. Clearly, the enemy had been surprised.

Cardy saw a small and bemused band of Germans appear with their hands up. At farmhouses near the landing fields, Dutch families waved to the air troops as they moved off. Somewhere, a piper was playing 'Blue Bonnets Over the Border', the regimental march of the King's Own Scottish Borderers.

Miller left the scene of his landing flattened on top of a jeep. His sten was ready, but opposition had not materialised by the time he reached the pilots' rendezvous in woods by a psychiatric institute. There, he joined others digging slit trenches in the sandy soil. It was laborious. After half an hour, Miller stopped for the ritual brewing of tea.

With him were Hollingsworth and Arthur Webb, a pilot invalided from flying duties who had begged the trip as a passenger. For a while they rested and refreshed themselves. 'Is this all there is to it?' asked Hollingsworth.

I 2

'Like a Hero'

SS Major Sepp Krafft, the 35-year-old commander of Panzer Grenadier Training and Reserve Battalion 16, gazed with horror from his headquarters in the Wolfheze Hotel, less than a mile from the glider landing fields. From the hotel, Krafft could actually see the aircraft on the ground, and the air troops, some 'a few hundred yards away'. He estimated the enemy to be three or four thousand strong. The strength of his own force—the only German troops in the vicinity—was slightly more than 300 men, two companies nearby, one at Arnhem.

Sick with apprehension, Krafft realised that the civilian population would 'surely side with the enemy and be particularly dangerous in the báttalion's rear'. For a moment he pondered the aim of the air landing, wondering if the target was Deelen, a German airfield not far away. More probably, decided Krafft, the Arnhem bridge was the objective. Should he, then, try to get his men there and defend the point?

He resolved, on reflection, to stay put. In any case, Krafft was convinced, he would be overwhelmed. Meanwhile, the best way to gain time would be to harass the British before they were fully organised. To this end, the German commander deployed his limited force in a line south from Wolfheze over something like a mile—all he could cover—halfway to the river's north bank. His men, he foresaw, must eventually be surrounded, but at least the enemy might be delayed in a thrust to the city's heart.

This scheme was approved by the town commander, Major-General Kussin, when he raced up to see what was going on. Astounded, he promised Krafft to find reinforcements somehow by evening, then returned to his staff car and roared away. Minutes later, Krafft heard a burst of machine-gun fire. Kussin lay dead on the Arnhem road.

Krafft called a driver. Ordering his possessions loaded into his own car, he commanded: 'Head for Germany. I don't expect to leave here alive.' It remained to make the most of his slim command. He had a number of temporary advantages. In the first place, the British would not know what strength was facing them. The major's men knew the thickly wooded area; where best to lie in wait. Machine-guns, he decided, should cover the roads while fighting patrols attacked through the trees. For a time, while the skymen found their bearings, they would be vulnerable.

Major Krafft had one material trump to play. For training purposes his battalion had been issued with a number of new missile launchers: multi-barrelled projectors which hurled formidable air-exploding mortar shells. Scattering shrapnel in wide areas, each discharge of the weapon gave the impression of several mortars being fired. The impact would soon be felt by the glider men.

Miller first heard the mortars as dusk approached. The sound erupted with a screech, like a car skidding, mounting to a screaming roar, then the explosion—each effect in triplicate. At the bottom of their trenches, the glider pilots felt the ground shake. They were starting to raise their heads when the process began again, to be followed by a third salvo of shrieks and thumps. When the noise subsided, Miller, clutching his sten-gun, peered through the darkening trees.

Something white was coming towards him in the woods. He alerted Webb and Hollingsworth. There were more figures, bobbing and flitting, each white-gowned. As the first drew near, he lowered his gun. It was an old woman. She was laughing eerily to herself, hitching her long robes. The inmates of the nearby asylum were being evacuated by the nursing staff. Silently, the air troops watched, filled with pity, as the group passed.

It was part of the bemusement which came with dusk. Men were dispersed now, about their own tasks, each wondering what was happening elsewhere. Mortars crashed; occasionally, bursts from small arms could be heard. To old hands, it was familiar: the spooky overture of violence. Krafft could see the Wolfheze asylum burning. His troops were still in action, but he knew he had been flanked and would have to try to fight his way east when darkness fell.

To the south, British paratroops had passed him on two roads. Under Lieutenant-Colonel John Frost, a Sicily veteran, the 1st Brigade's 2nd Battalion had marched on the bridge by the river road, while the 3rd Battalion took a road to the north of Frost. The advance of the 1st Battalion was by the railway line on Major Krafft's other flank. A special squadron in armed jeeps, led by Major Freddie Gough, had set out separately.

Where they were, how they had fared, Krafft no less than the glider men would have liked to know. In fact, no one to the west knew. Brigadier 'Pip' Hicks, commander of the brigade guarding the glider fields, had scant news. Unaccountably, the division's signals had broken down. Barely had the paratroop columns left for Arnhem when radio reception had begun to fade. In some cases, sets were out of contact with headquarters; other calls were unintelligible. So concerned was Urquhart at the lack of communication, that he had set out personally to locate Brigadier Desmond Lathbury, commanding the 1st Brigade.

It was the first serious snag for the landing force—a comprehensive one, for not only were the internal signals of the division faulty, special sets to call in close-support aircraft proved useless and contact with Nijmegen also failed.

Here, Chatterton, having landed General Browning, looked around for the other gliders with corps headquarters. One had hit a haystack, another the power cable for the district, but most had arrived intact. As the occupants moved off from the landing area, a flight of Messerschmitts straffed the Horsas, killing an RAF photographer who had gone back for a camera left in one ship. Disconcertingly, the sounds of battle had drawn near, but the sight of two American parachutists ambling casually past cheered the British group.

The first drop of Brigadier-General James M. Gavin's 82nd Division had landed near Nijmegen earlier. Many of its members had jumped with Normandy in their memories, bent on avenging the slaughter at St Mère Eglise. Some had hit the ground with their guns hot, having blazed at the Germans as they swung down. Now, part of the 5,000-strong American force engaged the enemy while others prepared to receive their gliderborne artillery.

Browning waited. Taking a tissue envelope from his pocket, the British general carefully extricated a small silk penant embroidered with the winged emblem of Pegasus and put it on his jeep. The noise intensified. By evening, shells were flying overhead and word arrived that the Americans were being pressed by German tanks. Gavin's paratroops needed the gliders urgently. Towards landing-hour, soldiers began heading for the zone as if, one put it, 'we were going to a football match'.

It was a fine evening, the sky clear. Suddenly, conversation was cut short by 'a great roaring sound, like a waterfall' and, coming in at less than a 1,000 ft, was 'a vast armada of Dakotas and Waco gliders', two gliders to each tug. Flak was bursting. Several of the tugs were hit, but they came on and, moments later, the Wacos were whistling down. It was, to Chatterton, a fantastic sight. The Germans had stopped firing to watch the drop. By dusk, the airborne howitzers were shelling the German guns.

Meanwhile, in Britain, the glider pilots due for Arnhem next day had watched the tugs returning from the first lift with rising hearts. Staff-Sergeant Gibbons had counted those at his own base. None was missing. On the radio, Gibbons heard the landings announced in news programmes. Opposition was said to have been light, a declaration celebrated at a party that evening in the sergeants' mess. Unusually, Gibbons remained abstemious.

At Down Ampney, south of Cirencester, glider pilot Desmond Page, among others, was confident. The stocky and ebullient Page had few worries. 'I was excited, looking forward to an easy op.' Delay next morning due to fog did not discourage him. As his Horsa lifted into uncertain skies, Staff-Sergeant Page was 'elated' to be going into action for the first time.

Gibbons and his co-pilot, 'Knappy' Knapton, had been to Normandy. Now, jeep and anti-tank gun behind them, they were well prepared. Both carried hand-grenades and fighting knives. Knapton had a rifle and a hundred rounds; Gibbons, a sten-gun and half-a-dozen magazines. Like all the pilots, they wore yellow identification scarves. It was still raining, a lot of cloud about. Knapton, slow with compliments, conceded that Gibbons handled the take-off decently.

Of 1,200 gliders marshalled for the second day, about 300 were British, bound for Arnhem. Until they got there, the gliderborne brigade could not abandon its defensive role at the landing zones to join the paratroops. Delay was therefore damaging. The worst weather was to the north, most gliders despatched several hours late by the southern route. Seven came down in England and two crews ditched. Gibbons, seeing ships around, thought they would be picked up.

Flak was somewhat more severe than on the first lift. Of 15 gliders forced down over Holland, three had their towlines cut by shell bursts. One tug was hit and the pilot killed. A wounded navigator took the controls and hauled the glider, itself damaged, back to the Allied lines, where it cast off. Though he had never landed an aircraft of any kind, the navigator then flew the tug back to England, touching down safely at Martlesham Heath, its base.

In many gliders there were casualties. Approaching Arnhem, George Betts saw his co-pilot, Staff-Sergeant Rickwood, slump badly wounded at the ship's controls. Taking the plane down, Betts did what he could for his comrade, but Rickwood died. Other pilots encountered fire, despite the efforts of Hicks's men, as they reached the ground. Stan Graham, Page's co-pilot, was the first to leave their own plane. A quiet and thorough man, he put his head through the door and asked Page to pass a rifle to him. Page clearly remembers replying, 'Why?'

'It was a damn silly question, but I was still complacent about the trip. I felt carefree, as if it were a glorified exercise. Stan said in his sober manner, "We're being fired at". I could hardly believe him. It scared me stiff.'

Like the pilots of the first lift, the newcomers met a varied, sometimes odd, scene. In Heelsum, villagers were at their gates as if to watch a carnival, pressing apples and drinks on the air troops. One man kept repeating in English how glad he was the Allies had come at last. 'It was almost pathetic. I began to feel like a hero,' a pilot wrote. Not far away, glider men crouching with members of the Dutch Resistance by a wood saw a small boy emerge with his hands raised. He had been sent, he said, by some Germans who wished to give themselves up. After a brief conference, the boy returned to tell the Germans to come out.

Other glider pilots found that their rendezvous was a home for the blind near Wolfheze. Oblivious to German sniper fire, a party of inmates assembled outside and began to sing the British national anthem. It was about four o'clock and Page, arriving from the landing zone, was torn between standing to attention and seeking cover, which seemed the wiser course. Stoically, the pilots remained upright until the recital stopped, then abruptly ducked. Soon afterwards, they were on the road already marched by the paratroops.

'I'd gone a mile or two,' Page recalled later, 'when I passed out. In my enthusiasm, I had tried to carry too much—two killing grenades, a smoke grenade, two PIAT bombs, a sten, twelve magazines, a dozen packs of ammunition in my shoulder-kit. They dumped me on a trailer to recover. I was still there when a sniper got the driver, jeep and trailer swerved, and I fell off.'

Des Page spent the night beneath a blanket beside the road.

Like most of the glider men, he had little idea what was happening elsewhere. Gibbons, in his diary, was noting at the same time: 'Am writing this in the dark; we are somewhere on the road to Arnhem; our leading columns have run into trouble and there is a bit of a battle going on . . .' It was as concise a summary of the situation as most participants could then have made.

Ian Toler had been impressed by the calm on Monday morning. The men on the landing fields had washed and shaved when Lieutenant-Colonel W. D. H. McCardie of the 2nd Battalion, South Staffordshires, announced that his companies were to move in support of the paratroops. Major Toler, whose pilots had flown in the Staffords, decided to stay with them.

Following the railway from Wolfheze towards Arnhem, his men formed a rearguard for the glider troops battling ahead to the main road. Here, in the afternoon, Toler and his pilots left the Staffords to swell the ranks of a parachute company. Oddly, as he recalled later, the Dutch people of the suburbs seemed unperturbed, going about their business quietly as the skymen advanced through them. Towards dusk, signs of heavy fighting lay over Arnhem, tracer and shelling evident. Scouting forward, Toler met an RAF squadron-leader on the street. His plane, a Stirling tug, had been shot down south of the river and he had crossed by the ferry, paying normally.

Again, the pilots went forward. It had grown dark, and bullets and mortar bombs flew over them. Beset by the mounting stench of exposed drains, they lay at last on the pavement, napping fitfully.

At about 2 a.m. they were called to a house where a candle burned. Grouped round the candle were McCardie, Lieutenant-Colonel David Dobie of the 1st Parachute Battalion, and a couple of other officers. The mood was grave. McCardie, it seemed to Toler, had aged since the afternoon. As Toler listened, he began to learn just how much had been going wrong.

Colonel Frost and the 2nd Parachute Battalion had overcome pockets of resistance on the river road, securing the north end of Arnhem bridge. But it was swept from the south by fierce gunfire, and attempts to cross it, though courageous, proved futile. Nor could other means be found to traverse the stream and shift the German guns. All Frost could do was occupy the houses on his own side and wait for reinforcements to come up.

Meanwhile, the 3rd Battalion had been split by unexpected opposition in the Oosterbeek suburb and the town itself. Ranged against its companies were armoured cars, self-propelled guns, mortars on a scale unpredicted by intelligence. Hard as the 3rd Battalion fought to reach Frost, it had not been able to do so by Monday evening. Indeed, its divided remnants were surrounded by a gathering enemy.

The 1st Battalion had encountered equally surprising strength. According to Dutch Resistance, few German troops had been in Arnhem at the outset. Yet Dobie's men were now confronted by tanks and half-tracks, with little fire-power to answer them. Blocked on the railway, the paratroops attempted to slip round to the south through gardens and back streets. Snipers and mortars savaged them. Finally, while Frost and his men hung on tenaciously, the mauled 1st Battalion was stopped in the northwest suburbs.

Elsewhere, it was the same tale. Gough's armed jeeps, ambushed by 20 mm guns and armoured vehicles, were forced to halt. It perplexed the crews. 'There were supposed to be only a few old grey Germans in Arnhem and some ancient tanks . . .' Gough had expected 'a pushover'. In fact, every thrust met ferocious force.

Urquhart, finding Lathbury at length on the Arnhem road, had watched mortar bombs falling brutally on the paratroops. One hit his jeep as the general crouched in a slit trench. There, on Sunday, the gravity of events was already clear. Lathbury had no contact with his 1st Battalion; only spasmodic linkage with Colonel Frost. Moreover, the foe was thick between Urquhart and the landing zones. Pinned down, without signals contact, Urquhart himself was impotent.

By Monday night, Frost and a diminishing band were still at the north end of Arnhem bridge, desperately signalling their need for help. Divisional headquarters, its radio silent, presumed them overwhelmed. McCardie knew otherwise. He had picked up Frost's call. If the bridge were not to be relinquished, he had to act. Now, as Toler joined them by candlelight, the two colonels were planning to lead their embattled sky troops to Frost's aid. Ahead, the Germans were reacting with weight and speed.

13

Killing Ground

The glider pilots assigned to protect divisional headquarters surveyed the white house. On the western fringe of prosperous Oosterbeek, the Hartenstein hotel had an air of country elegance. Its drive was smoothly gravelled, its lawns shaded by splendid trees. Rhododendrons flourished in the sandy soil. On one aspect was a pleasant fenced tennis court, the whole enfolded by deer-browsed parklands. Now, from a pole at the front, hung the Airborne divisional flag.

With some sense of desecration, the fliers were digging trenches in the clipped lawns. Miller and Webb, choosing a low bank which offered a good field of fire, laboured sweatily. Hollingsworth, some 20 yds away, had two prisoners digging for him. Other captured Germans were being herded on the tennis court. Nearby, a wooden hut contained a wash bowl and running water. It was crowded with begrimed men sluicing and trying to shave.

Refreshing himself, Miller filled his water bottle and an empty biscuit tin he had picked up, and returned to his slit trench. From the east, sounds of fighting indicated that the once-advancing air troops were falling back. The scream of mortar bombs sent the men to earth. When they rose, black smoke hung in clouds above the firs, and Miller's contemplation of the Hartenstein was tinged with doubt.

Three days earlier, the staff of Field Marshal Walter Model, one of Germany's most incisive commanders, had left the hotel hurriedly. Ironically, the hustling Model had picked Oosterbeek as a billet because it was a quiet place. The Arnhem sector had struck him as a tranquil one, of no particular significance save as an area for units in need of rest. For this reason, two weeks earlier, he had instructed his subordinate, General William Bittrich, to withdraw his battered armour, the élite 2nd SS Panzer Corps, to the Arnhem region. Bittrich had dispersed his force among the woods and villages a few miles north and east of the old city, carefully hidden from snooping planes. His men were not concerned with Major Krafft's few reserves. Their existence was scarcely known.

While the tanks of Bittrich's divisions, the 9th and 10th, were refitting, not all of them were immobilised. Moreover, the corps had a substantial number of other armoured vehicles—cars, troop carriers, self-propelled guns—which were serviceable, together with nearly 10,000 men.

When Model's Sunday lunch had been interrupted by British gliders landing just down the road, the field marshal had fled Oosterbeek so hastily he dropped laundry in the dash to his staff car. At first, he believed a raid was being mounted to get him personally. By the time he reached Bittrich at Doetinchem, the general's headquarters east of Arnhem, information about the landings was more elaborate and Bittrich already had units moving. Model was in his element. Bold challenges, the need for fast decisions, stimulated him. Phoning Von Rundstedt, Hitler's western supremo, for reinforcements, he sized the situation with Bittrich.

A remarkable stroke of information aided them. Far south, opposing the American landings at Eindhoven, was a man who had commanded air troops before the Allies had thought of them. By strange coincidence it was Colonel-General Kurt Student, the officer who had dreamed of taking London by glider assault, whose forces bore the brunt of the

US 101st Division's attack. At first, he was puzzled by the strategy. Then all was clear to him. Unbelievably, the complete Allied orders for Market Garden were found in a crashed Waco near his headquarters. By the second day of the operation, Model, too, knew the Airborne plan.

Ignorant of such developments, the air troops battling to reach Frost were stunned by the German strength. Wherever they turned, German guns and tanks were in position, sweeping streets, machine-guns hammering from vantage points. It was almost as if Arnhem were a prearranged killing ground, and they, the skymen, had stumbled into it. In the darkness remaining before Tuesday dawned, the remnants of McCardie's Staffords and Dobie's paratroops fought forward. Near them were what remained of the 3rd Parachute Battalion under Lieutenant-Colonel F. A. Fitch.

Daylight exposed them to the fury of the Panzer force. The carnage was terrible. A paratrooper who watched his friend dragged away with half an arm gone and an eye out, remembers bodies everywhere—in some cases, just parts of them adhering to doors and walls. 'I still wake up in horror, the sights coming back after nearly 40 years.'

Crouching, moving in short dashes, the men tried to keep going, but German armour blocked the roads, they were flayed by multi-barrelled guns and automatic fire. Both paratroop colonels were hit, Dobie wounded and Fitch killed. In the holocaust, their depleted units were reduced to clusters of desperate troops, confused and pinned in beleaguered corners. 'We kept trying to make it but it was a disaster,' recalled one of the 1st Battalion's 40-odd survivors. 'Then we seemed to be going backwards.'

Fighting beside them as they struggled to withdraw were glider pilots. Staff-Sergeant Les Foster was one of five who took cover in a damaged house. The Germans were across the road. Foster, in favour of lying low in the cellar, was outvoted, and they split up to look for firing positions in the several rooms. 'I had just returned from one of the upstairs rooms when I heard a shout from Charlie, who staggered out into the hall with his face covered in blood. I wiped away what I could and found that a bullet had scoured a deep furrow right across the top of his forehead taking a good part of the bone with it.'

Binding the wound, the others put the man on a bed with pillows round him. Later, he was wounded again as he was evacuated through a window, and a third time before leaving Arnhem. What struck Foster most vividly about the pilot was that he never stopped smoking a Meerschaum pipe.

At about five o'clock, the party heard the sound of tanks and saw one outside. Setting their PIAT on a table in the bathroom, they fired two bombs through the window. Both missed, but the noise caused the tank commander to raise his hatch and shout at the German infantry supporting him. Foster, with an easy target, fired his rifle and again missed. The yells of the Germans as they now attacked persuaded a British sergeant in a neighbouring house that the pilots had been overrun, and he hurled three grenades from an upstairs window into their building. Two were ejected before they exploded. The third went off, but harmed nobody.

Meanwhile, other glider pilots under Major Peter Jackson were repelling repeated attacks to dislodge them with flame-throwers and armoured vehicles. One officer, Tony Murry, was hit by a bullet which passed clean through his neck without killing him. At St Elizabeth's hospital, near the outskirts of the city, he encountered a bizarre situation. Surrounded by casualties, British and German medical teams were working side by side in the building while the battle raged outside. Two days after treatment, Murry walked out of the hospital, then behind the Germans, and managed to rejoin his besieged friends.

The residue of his squadron had been taken over by Tony Plowman, another officer. As the enemy attacked behind a barrage of mortar fire, Plowman rallied his few weary pilots and, brandishing a revolver, drove the Germans back. As a further gesture, he led a derisive chorus of 'Lilli Marlene', the German marching song, roaring 'Come and get her, you bastards!' at the end of it. He was wounded not long afterwards.

At the height of the battle, glider pilot Maurice Willoughby was amazed to see a party of senior officers, including Urquhart, scramble across a garden behind some buildings towards a high wall. Struggling to rejoin headquarters, the general was involved in fierce skirmishing, killing one German with his automatic. Beside him, Lathbury was hit and paralysed. As Willoughby watched, Urquhart made an unsuccessful bid to clear the wall. Suddenly, glider pilot Major John Hemmings appeared behind the general and, 'placing both hands firmly under his bottom', heaved him over.

Turning to Willoughby, Hemmings grinned. 'I'll dine out on this one for months,' he said.

Slowly, they were forced from Arnhem back through Oosterbeek. A ring was closing around the force. Beyond the Hartenstein, German units had seized the landing fields and were squeezing east towards the hotel. Staff-Sergeant Vic Wade was with other pilots entrenched by a wood when a tank trundled boldly across their front. To Wade's astonishment, two men doubled from the wood and pursued the vehicle. One was carrying a PIAT, the other its ammunition, both loads which made running very difficult. Closing on the tank, they threw themselves to the ground, fired their bombs and left it a useless hulk.

Wade's small party was later isolated by the Germans and fought doggedly outside the perimeter.

At some time on that fluid and shrinking front, Staff-Sergeant 'Carl' Carling was ambushed. With him on patrol, glider pilot McDonald was hit by Schmeiser fire. Side-stepping behind a tree, Carling peered forward to see the German with the Schmeiser advancing along the track. He was a youthful-looking soldier and, spotting Carling, fired from the hip. The burst missed. The German dropped to Carling's single rifle shot.

Enemy troops were all around now, and a bullet put

Carling's gun out of action. McDonald was lying face down, a ragged hole in the back of his battle smock. 'He looked very dead . . . I heard orders being shouted in German. Their commander was urging them to move in.' Grabbing McDonald's rifle, Carling lobbed a grenade in the direction of the German voice, surviving to reach his lines again. Years later, he was to meet McDonald in London. Somehow, McDonald had lived, given treatment by the Germans, to escape at length from an ambulance train.

Des Page was among a group of pilots under Lieutenant Ron Johnson which, reaching a cross-roads at Oosterbeek, dug in to form part of the perimeter near the Hartenstein. To the east, Frost's small band was still fighting at the bridge. Of Montgomery's Second Army, whose armour had been due at Arnhem hours ago, there was no word. 'Things looked bad, but we were too tired to speculate. It was the fifth time we had dug in, every time falling back.' Then, to the south, the pilots saw anti-aircraft shells bursting and, amid the blobs, a heartening sight: Horsas and Stirling tugs.

'My first reaction,' recalls one pilot, 'was "Thank God— reinforcements! At least they know we're in trouble." Then I wondered where the hell they were going to land.'

That morning, the third day, a single battalion of Polish paratroops under Major-General Stanislaw Sosabowski had been due to drop to the immediate south of Arnhem bridge, expecting it to be in British hands. Flying conditions had postponed the lift and, by evening, Sosabowski's parachutists were still in England. But a contingent of Poles and engineers with guns and heavy equipment had eventually taken off in 46 British gliders.

According to plan, they were to land north of Oosterbeek in a zone secured by troops put down by the first lifts. In fact, fierce fighting was taking place in the region as they flew out, the King's Own Scottish Borderers confronted by mounting force. As the gliders released, the landing fields were on the verge of being overrun by German arms.

Thirteen gliders had been lost on the flight from England. Three of these had fallen in the sea, five in Holland. In another, both pilots had been wounded but were flying on. Their fighter cover, misled by the altered timetable, had not materialised. Enemy planes were in the area and anti-aircraft fire was formidable. Looking down over Oosterbeek, the fliers had no idea what awaited them. Glider pilot Travis-Davison had found the briefing sketchy. Crews had been told 'that the situation was unknown'.

From the grounds of the Hartenstein, their fellow pilots watched tracer and shell bursts flail the sinking planes. The Horsas jerked uncomfortably. One, rolling over, plunged out of control behind the trees. Another shuddered, turning steeply as it was hit. The flaps came down and it dived earthwards, still manageable. Some caught fire as they were landing, their loads quickly abandoned by imperilled crews.

Around, the woods echoed and re-echoed the sounds of conflict. Trapped in the crossfire, confused by the terror and noise which greeted them, the Poles fired at both sides and, in the gloaming, were shot at by both in turn. Only three of the anti-tank guns came through safely, and few supplies. So dazed were the glider troops that many were captured on the spot. Next morning, their compatriots were to parachute to a reception even deadlier. Model's men, forewarned, picked them off as they floated down. Sosabowski, with less than half a battalion, was himself besieged.

By now, re-supply was an urgent need. To the RAF crews of 38 and 46 Groups, England-Arnhem was becoming a shuttle service. 'We knew the way; we had done four lifts so far.' What they did not know, and could not be told, was the constriction of Urquhart's force. It was decided, to ensure the supplies hit the planned zones, to approach at low altitude. The flak was furious. As the Dakotas of 46 Group flew over Oosterbeek at 500 ft, the Germans stopped pounding the perimeter and turned everything they had on the air fleet.

At the Hartenstein, glider pilots watched spellbound. Bob

Cardy was sharing a trench with Staff-Sergeant Wilkinson, a slim Australian who had gone to England for medical treatment, volunteered and been accepted for the army as A1. They were deafened by Dakotas and the blast of guns. 'It didn't seem possible the boys could fly through such a blizzard,' recalls Cardy, 'yet they were doing it—being shot from the sky, but coming on in streams. It was stupefying, inspiring bravery.'

One and then another went down, trailing flames and smoke. Flight Lieutenant David Lord's Dakota was hit on the run-in and caught fire. 'They need the stuff down there,' Lord told his navigator, Flying Officer Henry King, 'We'll go in and bale out afterwards.' They went in twice. On the ground, troops of both sides watch in awe as Lord turned for a second run, flames spreading, his despatchers toiling in the gaping door. Finally, there was an explosion and the plane crashed. King, the only survivor, found himself on Dutch soil, his clothes smouldering.

Behind the Dakotas came Stirlings of 38 Group. Glider pilots who had flown out with the big tugs raised a cheer for them, many men moist-eyed. Their chaplain, the Rev G. A. Pare, watched 'in agony'. More than one machine blazed. Wing Commander Peter Davis, the sailplane enthusiast who had been a friend of the glider men since Rock's day, flew in with a motor burning—almost certain disaster for a Stirling. Holding course until his cargo had been dropped, he climbed to give his crew height enough to bale out. In doing so, he stayed too long in the cockpit to save himself.

Below, the cheering had stopped. The first containers had floated wide. As more and more fell outside the perimeter it became clear they were being aimed unerringly at the northern supply zone. The RAF did not know it was in German hands. Tearing off yellow scarves, the glider pilots waved frantically, but the trees screened them from the air crews. Signal flares were lighted for the second drop, but without effect. For the most part, though some containers were recovered, the heroism of the airmen had been in vain.

The German barrage reverted to ground targets. From first light Tuesday, the sounds of battle had drawn nearer to the Hartenstein, shock waves of mortar bursts beating through the great trees. Then, as tea was brewed for a morning drink, glider pilots saw a jeep speed up to the hotel and a burly figure jump from it. General Urquhart had reached headquarters after a day and a half dodging Germans at pistol range. His message to Browning, if it could be delivered, was unambiguous.

'Casualties high. Resources stretched to utmost. Relief within 24 hours vital,' he ended it.

14

The Ring Closes

That evening, Tuesday 19 September, Brigadier Chatterton was present at a taut battle conference at Nijmegen. To the south, round Eindhoven, the American 101st Division had achieved its initial task of easing the way for the thrust north. The Wacos were doing a good job. About 1,900 would be used in the US sectors altogether, and the bulk so far lifted had shown its worth.

But at Nijmegen the Germans were contesting the bridges bitterly, pressing to seal General Gavin's force. So far, the 82nd Division's casualties were some 900, others missing or separated from the main groups. As the tanks of the Guards Armoured Division approached the Waal, the Americans were on the south bank; the Germans still controlled the vital bridge.

The thrust to Arnhem came to an abrupt halt. Not only was the river 400 yds wide, a further 200 yds of flat land was swept from an embankment beyond by German gunners. Eighty millimetre guns covered the bridge itself. Already, attempts to carry the crossing head-on had failed at high cost. Now, with every hour compounding the crisis for 'Market Garden', Gavin proposed a plan to the Allied commanders at the conference. The 3rd Battalion of the

American 504th Regiment, commanded by Colonel Reuben Tucker, should cross the stream in boats and assault the bridge from the German side while the tanks gave support from the Allied side.

It seemed a suicidal scheme. The troops would have to traverse the river in flimsy canvas boats with only smoke to screen them from the enemy, then advance 200 yds swept by German fire. The Guards officers looked at Tucker. His face was practically obscured by his helmet. He wore a pistol holstered under an arm, a knife strapped to one thigh, and he was sucking a fat cigar. Occasionally he took it from his mouth and, to the fascination of the Guards officers, spat juicily. They did not envy him.

For Chatterton the moment was dramatic. With the exception of the corps headquarters group at Nijmegen, virtually the whole of his force was at Arnhem: some 1,200 pilots. If they were lost, the Glider Pilot Regiment would be powerless. News of Urquhart, though scant, was bad. At least for one thing Chatterton could be thankful—the fighting skills of his pilots. He had picked them for their toughness and initiative, insisting on their training as complete combat soldiers.

Lack of such training for American glider pilots hampered Gavin. While many hundreds were in the area, they were primarily airmen with little preparation for a ground role. It was not their own fault. 'Despite their individual willingness to help,' said Gavin later, 'I feel that they were definitely a liability. . . . When the enemy reaction builds up and his attack increases in violence and intensity, the necessity for every man to be on the job at the right place is imperative. At this time glider pilots without unit assignment and improperly trained, aimlessly wandering about, cause confusion and generally get in the way.'

Chatterton's pilots were outstanding on the ground. As the situation at Arnhem deteriorated, many non-commissioned glider pilots assumed command of groups from other units. Glider pilot Regimental Sergeant-Major

Tilley took control of an infantry battalion when it had lost
its officers. Lieutenant-Colonel Murray, who had flown
Urquhart, was to replace the wounded Brigadier John
Hackett in command of the 4th Parachute Brigade.

Meanwhile, Chatterton and his companions pinned their
hopes on Tucker's men. At 2.30, Wednesday afternoon, two
squadrons of Sherman tanks moved up to the Waal and
began to pound the Germans across the stream. Half an hour
later, the first wave of Americans pushed their boats out and
paddled desperately with their rifle butts.

Some were gripped by the current and swirled in circles.
Some boats sank beneath the heavily weighted troops. Men
laden with grenades and ammunition could not swim. As the
small fleet dotted the river, the smoke screen covering it
parted, the German guns ranged in. In the words of a British
tank commander: 'It was a horrible, horrible sight. Boats
were literally blown out of the water. Huge geysers shot up as
shells hit and small-arms fire from the northern bank made
the river look like a seething cauldron.'

'I don't know how many hundreds went over,' wrote
Chatterton, 'but not many reached the other side.'

Those who did went forward like madmen through the
barrage, stopping only when they dropped or reached the
German posts. Frenzied by its losses and the sheer odds
against it, Tucker's 3rd Battalion spared nothing, clearing the
embankment towards the bridge. Suddenly, the watching
Guardsmen saw Americans at its far end. Germans were still
on the bridge and at the near end. With a roar, the tanks
charged them. Shells were flying, striking girders, rocking
the multi-span structure and the tank crews. Then, in the dust
and smoke, they met Tucker's men. Elatedly, British and
American troops embraced.

Arnhem was just eleven miles ahead of them. But they
were not clear. The road was mounted on polderland, flanked
by dykes. Armoured deployment was impossible, and
German guns covered the road itself. Without infantry
support, the tanks could not progress, and Gavin's force was

fully stretched to hold its own ground. The armour was forced to wait until the regiments it had outpaced slogged up to it.

Wednesday began at the Hartenstein hotel with mortar bombing and the call for medical orderlies. Glider pilots guarding the German prisoners, who had burrowed like moles in the tennis court, noticed a captured officer standing upright in his trench, head and shoulders above the rim. He did not duck as the bombs shrieked, but stared fixedly towards the perimeter as if his rescue was imminent.

Branches, torn from the trees by the explosions, lay everywhere. For some men, the trenches had become graves. A burnt-out jeep lay on its side, the smell of smouldering tyres heavy in the air. Hollingsworth had narrowly escaped the bomb which hit the jeep. Not far away, Bob Pavett, another pilot, was improving his sandy hole. More bombs fell as a group of pilots set off to patrol the woods.

That morning, Toler and Shackleton reached headquarters. They had been ordered to return by McCardie before his doomed attempt to reach Colonel Frost, and had found their way back with the Stirling pilot. For the first time in 72 hours, they washed and slept a little before being sent to hold a house southwest of the hotel. Advising the occupants to leave, they dug in there.

Lieutenant Johnson's pilots were holding another building on the perimeter, one side facing the station at Oosterbeek. At about the time the patrol was leaving the Hartenstein, one of Johnson's men was hit by a sniper. The pilot was dead. When a medical orderly, scrambling forward, was hit by the same marksman, their companions took action. Working their way to the house which held the sniper, they hurled grenades. 'We knew we'd got him when we heard him scream.'

Staff-Sergeant Gibbons, his position concealed with branches blown down by the mortar barrage, had breakfasted on tea and an oatmeal cube. The same morning, the

Germans almost overran his sector, but were driven back. 'My sten-gun jammed when I needed it most,' Gibbons recorded. 'Casualties mounting. No news has reached us of the 2nd Army.' Rumour had it that the tanks were at Nijmegen, but rumours were prolific and treated sceptically. Gibbons's section leader, Lieutenant Chittleburgher, had been killed. In a trench lined with blankets and an eiderdown from a Dutch house, Les Gibbons gave his sten an overhaul.

The headquarters patrol had set out by jeep, heads low. Drifting smoke obscured much of Oosterbeek, and the streets were empty, the men entrenched in the gardens or hidden indoors. Broken and mangled trees lay in the path. Beneath the trunk of one was the body of a paratrooper. The patrol was uneventful by Arnhem standards. Mortar bombs had seen it off. Mortar bombs had pursued it with spinning shrapnel on the perimeter. Mortar bombs welcomed it back to the hotel. In a wood, it had brushed with encroaching Germans. Their hold was tightening.

As the ring closed, the punishment it took increased in density. The din was constant—the shriek of mortars, stunning air-bursts, hum of shrapnel. German machine-pistols blasted raucously, a fast tearing sound. Heavier machine-guns, Mg 34s, thundered. 'The noise,' said one pilot, 'was mind-boggling. We had been trained for everything, small-arms and artillery. But nothing had prepared me for that continuous uproar. You could barely think.' To another pilot, 'it was bedlam. When it eased, my ears would whistle until it began again. I thought my eardrums were done for.'

In the afternoon, motorised Panzer units moved forward. Staff-Sergeant Page, in Johnson's party, was so close he heard the clatter of boots as the Germans debarked from trucks. For a while nothing happened, then, to the shock of the glider pilots, a half-track packed with infantry turned the corner and confronted them. 'Lieutenant Johnson got the driver with his revolver—they were that near. The rest of our blokes shot the others. After that, half the German army seemed to come at us.'

Model's reinforcements advanced with confidence. They had heard of a massacre at Arnhem, and that the remnants of the air troops were cut off. For Bittrich's divisions in particular, it was sweet revenge for their long retreat. They were precipitate. The battle near the station was typical. Johnson's men stopped two half-tracks with their PIAT and withdrew indoors to hold the infantry. Page recalls wondering at the smartness of the Germans, the gleam of the trappings on their uniforms. 'We looked like scarecrows ourselves, tired and unkempt. The first man I shot had a shining badge. Another seemed rather old; about 40, I imagined. He was in the act of throwing a stick-grenade. I let everything in my sten go at him.'

Ammunition was running short when Page felt a staggering explosion and the building shook. A German shell had swept a wall away. 'I reckoned then it might be all up for us. Just in case, I unstrapped my fighting knife and got rid of it. There was a notion that Hitler had ordered the shooting of prisoners caught with fighting knives. The Germans were still outside, but we counter-attacked and they fell back.'

It got quieter as darkness came. Behind the position a barn was burning. There was a cow inside, and one of the pilots ran to the building and turned the beast loose. Earlier, at the Hartenstein, another pilot had shot a wounded horse to end its agony. Now the flames from the barn increased tension, illuminating Johnson's spent force. Exhausted men felt for triggers as a door creaked. Page saw a figure come slowly from a dark house.

'It was a girl. She was carrying a bag and calling out that she was Dutch, but you could hardly see for the shadows and someone fired. It might have been a German, or one of our lads. She fell screaming, hit in the foot. Johnson ran to her. When he had brought her in, we bandaged her, gave her morphia, and I carried her to the aid post.'

Streams of wounded, soldiers and civilians, were being treated, some at posts hedged by German troops. One of the casualty stations, the Schoonoord hotel, alternated between British and German possession almost hour to hour. It was occupied by the crippled and dying of both sides. Others got attention at local aid posts, or in houses where Dutch families tended them. Soon, medical supplies were at low ebb. From another beleaguered aid post, the call for washing material was desperate. Glider pilot Betts, volunteering to carry soap through, was hit and became himself a casualty.

At night, British patrols looked for German guns. Derrick Shingleton was in a party of glider pilots led by Captain W. N. Barrie. Nearing their objective, they heard the tramp of boots and dived for the concealment of a garden. Shingleton recalls the moment vividly. 'The Germans, a large squad, halted and fell out on a grassy bank. They were so close we could have touched them. I was lying full-stretch, a flower of some kind in one nostril. How long we lay there without twitching I don't know. It seemed like hours. All the time, I thought I was going to sneeze.'

Beside him was Staff-Sergeant Reading, who shared the trench they had dug overlooking allotments near the Hartenstein. Now, as the Germans moved on, the pilots tried to locate the gun. It stood, they knew, in a copse near the town hall. Ghosting forward, they were forced to ground again by a burst of fire. 'Captain Barrie said he'd throw a grenade, but he was blasted as soon as he stood up. There was a screen of German infantry round the gun. We never could have got to it. Instead, we scrambled sideways through the trees and somehow found our way back along a lane.'

Four glider pilots, sent out on Wednesday night to find and secure the Rhine ferry south of headquarters, were faced with an equally hopeless mission. The intervening land was thick with Germans. Before long, they were under fire, one pilot wounded. Accompanied by eight volunteers from the South Staffordshires, they plunged on through thick woods and reached the river bank. There was no sign of the ferry at the point where it was marked on their battle maps. Nor, when they searched the curving stream for half a mile, could they find the craft. Most likely, someone decided, it had been sunk (in fact, it had lost its mooring and floated beyond reclaim). Every link with the south was being snatched from them.

Miller and Webb had sat talking in their trench after nightfall, a salvaged parachute over them to keep the chill out. Conversation turned on what, by now, was an obsessive theme: the Second Army, and why it had not arrived. They began to doze. At almost midnight, Miller awoke with a start. Webb was sleeping, breathing heavily. There was another sound near the headquarters.

'It was the noise of a heavy tracked vehicle moving around on the far side of the fir wood. A second seemed to be moving near it. Tanks! I knew *we* had no tanks of any kind.'

15

'*A Kind of Madness*'

In the mist of Thursday morning the tanks rumbled into action, met by glider-landed anti-tank crews firing over open sights. The dawn flare-up was shattering. Heavy German guns had joined the mortars, and Oosterbeek erupted in smoke and flames. Fast now, the once quiet suburb was becoming a rubble heap. At the battered Hartenstein, screams followed the arrival of shells and bombs, and 'an ache beat continuously' behind Miller's eyes. Webb's face, he noted, was lined with grime and weariness.

Many tough men, as the hours passed, would kneel and pray, among them Shingleton. 'It helped reconcile me,' he remembers, 'to the ordeal.' Another recalls a padre getting some pilots to sing with him. 'Anything to cheer us up a bit. We looked like souls from hell. You could see the same question in many eyes: how much more can we take of this? Then some small thing, a rumour maybe, would spark our hopes again.'

Thursday brought a wave of keen expectancy. Major Toler heard the news from an intelligence officer. The Second Army would be with them next day. Radio contact had been re-established with corps headquarters; relief was pressing north. Others received the same word. Passed along the perimeter, it raised ragged cheers. In trenches, woods and crumbling houses—wherever groups of dazed and bloodied men crouched—hearts rose, the will to fight surged. Johnson, wounded, was taken for aid, to return in bandages to his post. He was hit again, his pilots forced to move. They dug fresh trenches and held on.

In all sectors, glider pilots fought ferociously. On the western side of the perimeter, they were scattered among survivors of the Border Regiment, Royal Engineers, Poles and others. To the east, they fought beside remnants of parachute battalions and gliderborne artillerymen. In the north, they were among Scottish Borderers and more paratroops; in the south, with what remained of the Staffordshires. It was less a line than many outposts, held by small and often mixed bands of men.

German pressure kept it in constant flux. Page held three positions on Thursday. Forced from the station area to a sector manned by Scottish Borderers, he was digging in with other pilots when they were bayonet-charged. 'I was widening the trench. There was a terrific row and I looked up to see them coming through. We had to drop back, our flank overrun.' This time they entrenched with paratroops by a wood. Page's co-pilot, Graham, was still there; so was Staff-Sergeant Alan Poole, a glider pilot conspicuous for the yellow gloves he always wore. Page remembers him 'leaning over the edge blasting away with those gloves on. He always said he had cold hands.'

After dark, they moved to the bottom of a slope and dug in with the bank behind them. 'It seemed a good spot—until daylight. They were peering over the top, looking down at us. We could see their German helmets.' The pilots moved again.

At the Hartenstein, water was short, Thursday hot, and mouths were rough with grit from the sandy holes. Two of Toler's pilots were killed by mortar bombs, three wounded. The rest dug deeper, tearing doors and other pieces from the tennis pavilion to roof the trenches. On Gibbons's sector, fetching water meant braving sniper fire. Some of his companions had been killed by it. That morning Gibbons himself had dived for cover, landing in a sanitary trench. Filthy and stinking, he was bucked by word that the Second Army would soon tackle the Rhine crossing.

Indeed, some help was evident. Signals restored, Urquhart's officers had requested support from advanced batteries of Montgomery's artillery. It meant calling fire on the brink of their own positions, but the sky troops had been crucified too long by German fire to shrink from the risk of British shells. The support was accurate. Grimly, the defenders relished the sound of shell-bursts among German tanks.

Less accurate was a supply drop in the afternoon. Again, Stirlings and Dakotas came in doggedly; again, they paid the price, flaming aircraft plunging to the woods below. Once more, glider pilots watched coloured container chutes drift wide, white chutes billowing where crewmen had baled out. A few containers tangled in the trees around headquarters. Instantly, hungry men were climbing to cut the shrouds.

One container landed in the centre of the tennis court. Prisoners, hungry as their captors, dragged it eagerly to the guards. Mostly, the supplies proved worthless to Urquhart's troops. Another container fell near Gibbons. Rushing for it in hope of food, he found instead 'two 17-pounder shells, absolutely useless to us as all our 17-pounders are out of action.'

Glider pilot Sergeant Read recalled consolation a while afterwards. With Staff-Sergeant Atkins, his flying mate, he was helping to hold a house on the northeast of the perimeter when a German supply lorry took a wrong turning and drove towards them. Knocking out the crew, they captured the contents, including a stock of German cigarettes. They were malodorous, but Read inhaled gratefully.

Despair for supplies was accompanied by bitter news. Early on Thursday, even as hopes were roused at Oosterbeek, Frost's heroic bridge party had been overwhelmed. Down to less than 100 effective men, their ammunition almost spent, the force had long since lost count of its maimed and dead. More than 200 wounded, including Colonel Frost, lay in the cellar of one building, and that, by Wednesday evening, had its roof on fire. Ordering Gough, who had joined him, to hold on with fit men in other buildings, Frost sought a truce before the casualties incinerated. He was just in time. Blazing timbers were falling as the Germans helped pull the wounded out. Gough carried on, but in the first hours of morning was overrun.

With all possibility of holding the bridge gone, the division's cardinal function had now ended. At Oosterbeek, only the survival of the enclave remained a purpose, optimism a spent force. Wrote Gibbons: 'We have already had too many false hopes.' By Friday, the day of promised relief, despair was justified.

That morning, the Guards armoured column was still blocked near Nijmegen by German guns which dominated the highway and its ditched flanks. On the other hand, Bittrich's tanks were on the move south. Now rolling without hindrance over Arnhem bridge, they posed a growing threat to British infantry slogging north. In fact, one British unit had reached the Rhine. In a daring sprint through misted side lanes, scout cars of the 2nd Household Cavalry had reached Sosabowski's beleaguered Poles on the south bank, to be followed by a British armoured squadron. But it was too slight a force to turn issues. Sosabowski failed in a brave bid to cross the stream.

Of 10,000 airborne troops landed at Arnhem, the division now numbered, by Urquhart's estimate, less than 3,000 fighting men. They were hungry, dirty, battle-weary. Some roamed the enclave in a state of shell-shock. One wandered naked and babbling. Glider pilot Edward Mitchell was stationed near a paratrooper who ran amok, firing indiscriminately before taking his own life. Bob Cardy was crawling to the Hartenstein for water when mortar bombs hit the hotel again. Tumbling into a trench, he found two of his pilot friends there. 'Suddenly, one fixed his bayonet and shouted that he was going to get the bastards. We had to sit on him until he quietened down.'

Cardy knew how the man felt. His own trench-mate, the Australian glider pilot Wilkinson, had been killed by an explosive bullet in the groin. Another pilot had dropped dead in front of Cardy, hit by a sniper's bullet. Few men had not wondered when their time would come. Beside a path at the Hartenstein, Vic Miller heard a soldier muttering repeatedly, 'It's no good, we've had it; it's no good'. The man was begrimed and tattered, his eyes red-rimmed. Miller tried to cheer him, without success.

Around the perimeter, an insidious sense of being alone, left to cope single-handed, was taking hold. Often, the situation was exactly that. George Betts, hit in the thigh and foot by a mortar explosion that had blown his only companion, a young paratrooper, to smithereens, was surrounded by Germans. Crawling to the cellar of a house, he found himself with a Dutch couple and their daughter, a frightened little girl. Apologising for his intrusion, he lay on a pile of coke. The woman mopped his wounds with a scrap of petticoat.

Soon, they heard troops in the rooms above. Betts gripped his gun, a Schmeisser picked up from a dead German. Apprehensively, the Dutchman went upstairs. 'Suddenly,' recalls Betts, 'I heard a German voice shouting from the top of the cellar steps: "Kommen out, Tommy." I knew the Dutchman had reported me.' Betts understood. It was his capture against the lives of the frightened family. Hiding his gun under the coke, he staggered to the steps and gave himself up.

Glider pilot Lieutenant Michael Long was confronted on the northern sector by a German with a machine-gun. Long had a pistol. His shot caught the German's ear, then the pilot fell, hit in a leg by the responding burst. Before he could recover, his adversary was sitting on him. They bandaged each other's wounds before Long was led away.

Desperation redoubled the defiance of the dwindling force. 'It was as if,' recollects another pilot, 'we got a kind of mental second-wind as hope faded, a sheer bloody-minded determination to take the other side to hell with us.' For two days, Staff-Sergeant Wade's section was cut off from the division, encircled by German troops. There was no wireless contact. It received no orders. Wade and his fellow pilots simply waged their own war.

Elsewhere, Gibbons was trying to find food. His breakfast on Friday had been a couple of biscuits from a dead man's pack. Now, leaving an empty house with some provisions, he was knocked unconscious by a shell-burst. Coming round, he found one of his hands pierced by shrapnel and a pain near his heart where spent metal had failed to penetrate. The regimental aid post did not appeal to him. The doors and windows had been blown in; the roof gaped. Everywhere seemed 'splashed with the blood of friend and foe alike'. Returning to his trench, he discovered the result of a direct hit. His companions had gone. The next trench was deserted. It was evening. All he had eaten were the biscuits and some apples he had picked up. Gibbons took shelter in a house, his sten at readiness.

That night, Sergeant Read heard German voices calling for stretcher-bearers. Some glider pilots on his right had mounted an impromptu offensive in their area. For a while he slept, awakening as German infantry attacked his post. The pilots held them off. 'Then they brought up a self-propelled gun. Our PIAT struck the chassis but the undamaged gun retaliated by shelling us out. All our section hit by shrapnel were sent to the RAP.' Read, like Gibbons, did not linger at the aid post. Joining the remnants of a parachute brigade, he prepared to defend yet another line.

Des Page was about 50 yds from the enemy. Half a dozen glider pilots were entrenched with him on Friday, faces rough with stubble, some blood-stained. They were listening to dance music. 'I couldn't believe it. I think it was Joe Loss's band. It was coming from somewhere on the German side.

We just stared at each other, blear-eyed. At that stage, not much would have surprised us, but music did.'

Loudspeakers had joined Model's armoury. For a while the incongruous melody continued, then the record stopped and a voice blared in English: 'Gentlemen of the First Airborne Division, you are surrounded. Montgomery has bitten off more than he can chew. You have no chance. You have fought bravely, now save yourselves. Come out with your hands up.' There was a hush. At last, from somewhere in Oosterbeek, a rough voice rejoined: 'Bollocks, you stupid bugger! Why don't you piss off?'

Bob Cardy heard the appeal near the Hartenstein. 'By now we were getting few instructions, just doing the best we could. We knew we were encircled without the Germans telling us, but this van kept sending messages: "You've done all you can. Remember your wives and sweethearts back at home." We blasted it. That was the end of the smooth words.'

The Germans pressed again. When the deer park adjoining headquarters came under siege, glider pilots ran to face the breakthrough. Flinging themselves to ground at the edge of the hotel gardens, they tore at bushes to clear a field of fire. The view revealed was a macabre one. Line on line of blanket-wrapped bodies lay on the shell-pocked earth ready for burial. The area had been picked as the divisional cemetery. Events had overtaken plans to inter the dead.

Beyond the corpses, Germans were advancing from the Arnhem road, crouching and sprinting alternatively. Staff-Sergeant Miller could hear them bawling. He fired and saw a man drop. He kept firing. The other pilots were blazing with stens and rifles. A bren was thundering. The Germans stopped and ran back to cover, dodging clumsily. 'Suddenly,' recalls Miller, 'I felt tired, terribly tired.'

Candles lit the casualty post in the hotel's cellar. It was crowded. Wounded men covered so much of the floor that the doctors could scarcely move among them. The gloom reeked of antiseptic, and soldiers moaned. Arthur Webb, the pilot who had flown to Arnhem as a passenger, found himself among the injured. Crouched in his trench as a shell burst, he had felt a searing pain in an arm and his sleeve had turned deep red. Another shell victim lay on his stomach, back flayed, blood coagulating round the shrapnel wounds.

Increasingly, the hotel was straddled by German shells. Glider pilot Louis Levy was in his trench when the sky was blotted by debris and the fumes of burnt explosive filled his throat and nose. Raising his head, Levy saw a smoking crater stretching to the lip of Miller's refuge, which had caved in. He called, 'Are you OK, Dusty?' and Miller crawled from engulfing sand. He was safe, but his sten had been twisted like Plasticine.

Amid the terror, freakish incidents impressed memories. Miller recalled his stupefaction as a head of long blonde tresses rose from a trench, then an unmistakably female figure. Bearded faces gawped as the girl smiled uncertainly. She was pleasantly plump, less embarrassed than the pilot who escorted her, Staff-Sergeant Joe Clarke. His companion, a German servicewoman on leave in Arnhem, was thought to have seen too much to be returned to her own lines. Clarke had been detailed to watch over her.

On the perimeter, glider pilots were taking charge of other details. In many places, groups of bewildered men, sometimes lone soldiers without leadership, looked to the pilots for initiative. 'It wasn't just their stripes,' explained an infantry private, 'it was a kind of infectious sod-the-consequences madness which got you going when you were paralysed. It must have been flying those wooden coffins—they were ready to tackle anything.'

Lance-corporal Sydney Nunn of the 1st Air Landing Brigade recalled his encounter with a glider pilot who addressed him genially as 'old lad'. They were in the copse with a 60-ton Tiger tank in front of them. Nearby was an anti-tank gun, but its crew had been knocked out. Nunn had no idea how to use the weapon. Undismayed, the pilot suggested they should crawl to it. As they did so, the tank opened up at them. Trees and branches were falling as they reached the gun. The pilot looked at it. 'I hope this thing works,' he told the corporal. Sighting hastily, the pilot pulled the trigger. The tank erupted in flames. Solemnly, the pilot shook hands with the astonished Nunn.

Many times, glider pilots demonstrated their versatility. Trained to use all the equipment gliders carried, they fought as makeshift gun crews, machine-gunners, PIAT and mortar teams. Repeatedly, they led small bands of survivors to clear Germans from their ever-encroaching posts, or to challenge tanks and self-propelled guns. Beside them, parachutists and glider troops refused to quit. Remorselessly, they were plastered with shells and bombs. Lieutenant-General Bittrich, whose men attacked bravely and persistently, had 'never seen men fight as hard as the British at Oosterbeek and Arnhem'. It was Saturday.

16

Exeunt

Looking back, everything had been wrong at Arnhem. They had been put down too far behind the enemy; the landing fields were too remote from the objective; the spread of the lifts over several days had been wrong. While intelligence had seriously underestimated the German strength, particularly in armour, predictions for the advance of the British armour had been sanguine. The maximum life of a lightly-armed air division behind the enemy in Holland had been put at four days.

Sunday, 24 September, saw the battle in its second week. It was the birthday of two glider pilots. Sergeant Leonard Overton was 22. His comrades brewed tea in a can of rainwater and wished him 'Many happy returns' with the first sip. He had nothing to eat that day; it was his only drink. Sergeant Read later recalled his birthday present: three hours of constant mortar fire.

The barrage was pitiless. Les Gibbons wondered if it was heavier than usual, or merely seemed so because resistance was running low. Everyone's nerves were stretched. At one stage Gibbons was searching for a sniper when he found a piano in a deserted house. Playing a few notes on impulse, he was rudely silence by his startled mates. His injured hand throbbed. Hundreds of more seriously wounded needed proper care.

So swamped by Sunday were the casualty stations that medical officers arranged a partial truce while their worst cases were evacuated to hospital behind the Germans. For two hours in the afternoon the barrage slackened to allow red cross vehicles to shift some 450 wounded from the area. Then the battle continued with renewed vehemence.

By now Model, countering fresh American glider landings in the southern zones, was battling for a stranglehold on the Allied corridor between Eindhoven and Nijmegen. He required, he told Bittrich, 'a quick finish to the British at Oosterbeek'. To glider pilot Page, now the senior of 17 men in a row of houses near the Hartenstein, it seemed that 'all hell was loose'.

That morning, in his previous position, he had counted six tanks with German infantry coming towards the post. For a while the small band of skymen held out, then they were forced to run. With another pilot, Tommy Snell, Page scrambled to a house and found the cellar. It was full of Dutch civilians. 'We left hurriedly. The Germans were still coming. Sprinting down a road, we dodged through some gardens and got into the houses by the hotel. The Germans occupied the houses across the road. We took stock.'

Page had munched raw potatoes but was 'too nervous to think much about food'. The taps in the house were not running. He skimmed some water from a bath and quenched his thirst. It grew cold. There was a woman's fur coat in one room. Putting it on beneath his smock, he waited at the window for the next attack. 'I thought that before Monday was through we would have had it—they would have killed or captured us.'

By Sunday night, General Urquhart's assessment was not dissimilar. Unless the relieving forces made physical contact early Monday it was unlikely, he concluded, the division could fight on. 'All ranks now exhausted,' he wrote. 'Lack of rations, water, ammunition. . . . Even slight enemy offensive action may cause complete disintegration.' Help was nearer than at any time, but a swirling barrier, the Rhine, frustrated the contact for which Urquhart called.

Advanced troops of the 30th Corps were actually on the south bank that Sunday, waiting for assault boats. Then came fateful news. Model had severed the corridor south of Nijmegen. With the Americans facing German reinforcements of increasing strength, strategic emphasis swung from Arnhem to the southern zones. That night, instead of crossing to reinforce the defensive ring, a few hundred troops of the 4th Dorsets embarked in small boats under orders to help Urquhart pull out. They stood little chance. Snatched by the current, swept by German guns covering the river, more than half of them were lost in the brave attempt. Few got through to the perimeter.

At 9.30, Monday morning, Field Marshal Montgomery sanctioned the proposed withdrawal of the 1st Airborne Division from Oosterbeek. Its strength was now less than 2,500 men. The enemy was at the gates of its headquarters and, together with a quarter-mile-wide river, straddled the line of escape south. The dawn was sombre, bringing rain clouds. At the hotel the entrenched pilots braced themselves. A bren was firing from the trees by the pavilion. Rifles cracked continuously, and the sound of Schmeissers was immediate. One of the captured Germans, a black-uniformed sergeant-major, had climbed from his hole on the tennis court to peer through the surrounding wire. Suddenly, he began to shout that prisoners were present. '*Kriegsgefangener hier!*' he bellowed urgently.

At that moment, Staff-Sergeant Miller saw a German soldier half rise from the trees dragging a machine-gun. Miller fired. A sten was firing nearby. The German pitched sideways and sprawled in the undergrowth. German and English voices were shouting. Recalls Miller: 'I saw three more camouflaged Germans bent double, dodging among the trees, and fired again. Then they were gone. Almost as fast as the firing had built up, it petered out.'

In the row of houses occupied by Page and his companions . a grim game of tag took place. It burst back and forth as fortunes of the moment changed. Peering cautiously from a window, Page found himself staring into the surprised face of a German leaning from a window of the next dwelling. Page ducked in, and the skymen planned quickly to clear the house. 'We got them out without loss to ourselves, then waited for the next move.'

Wade's group had fought through Saturday and Sunday completely cut off. Finally, on Monday, it was decided to try to make contact with brigade headquarters through the German lines. Two officers and a staff-sergeant, glider pilot Louis Hagen, volunteered to go. They were successful, returning mid-afternoon with orders that the unit was to withdraw through the enemy after dark. Meanwhile, the men should reduce fire so that its cessation would not alert the Germans to their retreat. They were among the first to get instructions for the night's work.

Urquhart's plan demanded secrecy. If the Germans suspected what was happening, it could not succeed. As the units pulled out in the darkness, scattered men would stay behind firing sporadically, emulating expected activity. Troops farthest from the Rhine were to move first, joined by others as they funnelled through the Germans to the riverside. There, if all went well, two companies of Canadian engineers would meet them with ferry boats. Orders were to be issued at the latest time consistent with the tasks involved.

Among the first to be informed was Lieutenant-Colonel Iain Murray, the glider pilot leader, now also commanding what remained of the 4th Parachute Brigade. Murray's pilots had been picked for an important task. They were to scout the columns through the enemy, and to act as guides along the dark paths. One of the first to learn the news from Murray was Major Toler. To mark the occasion, both officers shaved, Toler using Murray's razor and a dab of his shaving lather.

Glider pilot Captain Walchli sent for his flight at dusk. The rain had set in and about a dozen men appeared from the gloom around the hotel. Shells were dropping. The pilots ducked. 'Keep your mouths shut,' he said between explosions, 'but we've had it; we're pulling out.' They listened silently as he explained that they would be spaced as guides on the first lap from the hotel. Other pilots would be posted at distant points. Only when the last men were through would they leave their stations. 'Then we beat it,' Walchli said pithily.

The irony of their final assignment was evident. Operational orders for Arnhem had stipulated the withdrawal of glider pilots from the battle area at the first chance. Nine days after landing, they were being told they would be among the last to leave.

It was 8.50 when Walchli's men moved out. The rain was lashing. Apart from the flash of shell-bursts and the fitful glow of burning buildings, it was pitch dark. They had pulled socks over sodden boots, blackened faces already grey, and they talked in whispers when they had to speak. Every 50 yds or so, Walchli dropped a man off. Before the rest had gone two paces he was lost in the weeping murk. The first retreating contingents were due at 10 o'clock.

At that hour, Staff-Sergeant Wade and his beleaguered comrades left their posts and gathered in the shelter of a hedgerow. Waiting to quit had seemed a nightmare. A German sniper had homed in on the position, and the thought of being hit at the last moment was unbearable. Covering one side of the post with a bren-gun, Wade and a fellow pilot had exchanged reassurances from time to time. 'OK?' one would ask, and the other would ask in turn, 'OK?' At last, they were moving out.

For Bob Cardy, the thought of leaving the wounded was terrible. 'There were hundreds of them, many dying, including glider pilots. They could never have been got out. But it wasn't a nice feeling, going without your mates.' In fact, some wounded were taken on the withdrawal, despite orders. Medical staff remained with the rest to await the

Germans. Glider pilot padre the Rev. Pare, ignorant of the plan, was with the sick when it went ahead.

Other glider men were among those left in covering positions. At 6 o'clock an officer had scrambled to Page's house and told him not to pull out his men until midnight. They had decided 'to leave as a bundle when the time came, and scram fast. It would be too late for text-book retirements.' Gibbons was due to leave his post at 24.30 hours. As the evening drew damply on, punctuated by intermittent explosions, Gibbons hunched deeper in his trench and began to doze.

In teeming rain by a farmhouse on the line of retreat, Vic Miller shivered. Two shells had dropped near him, the blaze of shrapnel luminous. He had dived beneath a wrecked jeep. Now he waited for the first of the withdrawing columns. His feet, when he moved, crunched on broken glass. Across the farmyard a hay-rick smouldered in the downpour. It was a quarter-past-ten, 15 minutes after the leaders should have come through. Miller's misgivings grew.

Shingleton felt no happier. The big staff-sergeant had been one of 12 glider pilots called to the Hartenstein to act as scouts. Their job was to lead retreating parties by chosen paths to the river bank. They did not expect an easy night. Visibility was arm's length. Near the stream, on open ground, they might be silhouetted by flares and fires, and 'if the Germans spotted us, that was that'. His first party, South Staffordshire glider troops, hunched in the rain, waiting silently. Rags and socks wrapped their boots. Some were bandaged. Faces were gaunt and tense.

Despite the weather, Vic Miller was sweating now. Then a figure was outlined by the glowing rick. As the man advanced, Miller saw to his relief that he was British. Quietly, the glider pilot pointed the way ahead. The line of drenched and stooping troops which filed through was accompanied by a nerve-racking crunch of glass. Then they had vanished and waited for the next batch.

Sergeant William Thompson, another glider pilot, had the

same job. As the files ghosted from the night and disappeared again, shuffling slowly from the perimeter, it struck Thompson they were vacating a kind of massive abattoir. As yet, they were far from safe. Shells were falling, sending them to earth in snaking columns; machine-guns pounded on fixed lines. The German activity was fortuitous—so far the retreat had not been rumbled, but the river was still to come. The rain and wind increased.

An hour passed and men kept arriving at the guide points. They came in twos and threes and in dozens, some supporting crippled comrades, clutching weapons of many kinds. Then the flow began to dwindle until, finally, the pilots were alone again. Collecting his men, Walchli started south. Firing to the flank told of skirmishing. The woods were black—so dark that the pilots held each other's smocks for fear of parting company. Later, the trees behind, they lay flat as German flares soared. It was 1 a.m. At short intervals, tracer streamed from Bofors guns. Their purpose was to mark the limits of the crossing by repetitive bursts from the south bank. On the north side, shadowy queues were forming for the little boats. Slowly, the queues grew. Already, craft had been sunk or swept downstream, and those that remained were not built for large loads. Men shuffled anxiously. Come dawn, the ferries would have to stop.

Des Page and his men left the houses at midnight, flattening themselves as mortar bombs burst on the green outside. Several of the party were lost at once. 'To make things worse,' recalls Page, 'we went the wrong way. I led them straight towards the Germans and we had to turn tail and run like mad. Despite the rain, a lot of houses were burning. Germans were shouting. We didn't stop. There was a hell of a lot of noise, and fires everywhere.'

While they plunged through the woods towards the river, Gibbons awoke suddenly in his trench. He was alone. As he slept, the men in the neighbouring trenches had pulled out, unaware that they were leaving him. A one-man force in the line, he now left hastily, relieved to run into some paratroops. Together, they pushed through the dripping night.

For others, the withdrawal had become an endurance feat. Glider pilot Wade, crawling and tramping for two hours, had lost many companions on a ghastly trip. Shingleton was all-in. He had led two parties to the stream, returning for a third group. It was getting late. Fires were reddening the sky as he threaded dykes to avoid outlining the men behind. 'At the river it was tense. Wounded were being helped to the front; others felt they'd never make it. A boat would leave, dissolve in the murk and might not return. Understandably, those left were an edgy bunch.' His job complete, he moved away and sat down at the water's edge.

Many fugitives risked the swim. Some reached the far bank; others disappeared in the strong current. More than one crawled ashore in the dark to find himself still on the north side. Shells were falling near the tail of the column as Miller gained a boat at last. He thought it would sink beneath the weight aboard. Miller recalls the bosun, a Canadian, asking who could row and not getting one reply in the negative. But nothing happened when they did row. The boat was grounded fast by its excessive load. Cursing, a massive glider pilot jumped out, put his shoulder to the prow and heaved the craft free.

Elsewhere, there was good humour. Cardy remembers someone shouting, 'Seats at one and sixpence; ninepence standing', and found himself heading for the far bank. Gibbons heard a voice call, 'Any wounded?' A paratrooper, spotting his bloodstained bandage, pushed him forward. 'There was no panic, the others held back.' Men were swimming around the boat, bombs from mortars bursting as they set off. Page arrived at a breakwater in time to board a pontoon with an outboard motor. It struck the bank as it pulled away and he was pitched out. 'Someone yanked me in again. I was still clutching the Schmeisser I had picked up.' Read, ferried by the Royal Army Service Corps, found a military policeman directing men through the mud on the south shore.

By dawn hundreds of men had crossed the river—2,163 members of the original force eventually reached the far side—but hope was slight for those left behind. The Germans, now alerted flayed the stream and pressed forward. Staff-Sergeant Griffiths, the glider pilot and army boxer, reached the river after fighting his way from the perimeter. As the enemy closed in, he led a weary band, mostly Scottish Borderers, to try to hold the bank. Others were resisting in houses and nearby woods. Germans were everywhere.

'I saw one toss a grenade into a building. A hand appeared from somewhere and lobbed it out. It was like watching a cricket match. For a while we held them, but we had no chance.' Down to seven men of the fifteen who had followed him, Griffiths was ambushed near the riverside. One of the seven was ripped in half by automatic fire. The survivors, trapped against the water, gave themselves up. Griffiths hurled his empty rifle in the stream.

Including prisoners-of-war, 730 glider pilots were lost or wounded at Arnhem, more than half those involved in the operation. Many who got to safety could scarcely believe their luck. Derrick Shingleton had sat exhausted by the river when his night's task was done, with small hope for his own escape. Suddenly, there was a rustle in the shallows and an unmanned boat drifted into view. He clambered aboard. It seemed a miracle.

17

Mountain Scenery

'Market Garden' produced 13,000 casualties among Allied airborne troops and air crews, and established, in the words of one commentator, 'a 50-mile salient leading nowhere'. Arnhem had spelled disaster, the Rhine remained a barrier, and if there was a profit side to the operation few were agreed on it. In the outcome, one aspect of the venture was frequently overlooked. The glider landings, unprecedented in scale, had been a huge success.

Between them, British and American gliders had carried nearly 14,000 troops to battle, together with 1,690 vehicles, 290 guns and 1,260 tons of supplies and ammunition. Flight and landing losses had been relatively low. Commenting on the British operation, Urquhart observed that 'the landing of gliders was first-class. It was truly the most successful and accurate of any previous achievement either in operations or exercises. All units were able to move off to their tasks practically at full strength.'

That they returned tragically depleted was a particularly stunning blow to Britain's glider pilot force, for the training of pilots was a long job and could not replace the operational experience of those lost. Nevertheless, in a mere six months the Glider Pilot Regiment was to return to the Rhine, strength revived, for a reckoning which brooked no repulse. In the greatest single air landing of any time, the glider men would have their revenge.

Meanwhile, their fortunes varied. Bob Cardy found £40 waiting for him when he reached England. He had forgotten winning it at poker on the eve of his Arnhem flight. Derrick Shingleton celebrated his return by cabling his WAAF fiancé: 'Getting married on Monday—what are you doing?' Happily, she took the hint. Staff-Sergeant Des Page got back wearing the fur coat he had picked up at Arnhem to keep warm. He took care of it. Long afterwards, when the war was over, he traced its owner, went to Holland and returned it with his gratitude.

Other pilots, less fortunate on the retreat, escaped afterwards. A number were among more than 100 skymen who hid from the Germans, crossing the Rhine to safety that autumn in a triumphant group. A glider pilot chaplain, the Rev W. R. Chignell, reached the river with 20 wounded men and got a boat across. His colleague, the Rev Pare, having helped to comfort casualties, collected information and messages from captured glider pilots and jumped from a hospital train bound for Germany. For months he eluded recapture, sometimes posing as a deaf mute. Once, he hid in a shooting lodge while SS men searched the neighbourhood. They tried the door but, finding it bolted, were satisfied. Pare eventually reached Allied lines.

Staff-Sergeant Betts made a vain attempt to escape, hindered by an injured foot. Soon after the retreat he was able to help an airborne officer, Major Anthony Deane-Drummond, in his own successful bid. For 13 days Deane-Drummond hid in a cupboard at a villa where Betts was held prisoner. The glider pilot smuggled water and bread to him.

John Griffiths was held at Muhlberg, eastern Saxony, as Russian forces approached the prison camp. With glider pilots Ron Garnham and Ted Rolph, he climbed the wall and seized a Mercedes staff car. When that let them down, they piled into an Opel and drove hundreds of miles across

Germany before reaching an American unit fighting near Darmstadt. The war was then in its final days. Griffiths, a regular soldier, became one of the last men to fly a military glider before he switched to powered aircraft.

Glider pilot Paul Bazalgette was on leave in Kashmir when he heard the news of Arnhem on his radio. He had taken a houseboat on Dal lake, one of the most beautiful places he had seen, and was 'feeling a heel, having the time of my life while other glider pilots were on the spot'. Formerly an artilleryman, Lieutenant Bazalgette had been among a number of army fliers dispersed abroad after the Sicilian episode to form or join 'independent' squadrons. Flying gliders often salvaged from past campaigns, their activities beyond the orbit of the home force made up in exotic colour what they lacked in limelight.

Bazalgette had returned to North Africa after his battle-landing at Syracuse, then sailed for India. There, at Chaklala, an aerodrome near Rawalpindi, a few Horsas forming the nucleus of what was to become a joint army and air force glider wing in preparation for the invasion of Malaya and stations east. Wingate's glider chiefs, Cochran and Alison, had envisaged glider fleets spearheading the expulsion of the Japanese from the Eastern theatre, but there were few glider pilots now in India.

Armed with a roving commission, Bazalgette found himself scouting Calcutta, Bombay and Madras for likely trainees. They were to fly amid breathtaking backdrops: the Himalayas, the historic hills of the Northwest Frontier, Kipling country. Once, Bazalgette piloted a Horsa behind a Halifax for 1,200 miles from Rawalpindi to Dum Dum, half of India spread below. Many 'independents' gazed on majestic scenes.

Cornelius Turner looked down from his glider on Yugoslavia's Dinaric Alps. Captain Turner had left Bari, Italy, flying one of three Wacos with British glider pilots and American C47 tugs. Their mission was to land a team of

Russian officers, headed by Generals Korneyev and Goskov, in the foothills between Zagreb and Sarajevo, where Tito's guerrillas were holding out. Turner thought it must be an important trip. To divert the Germans, 50 Flying Fortresses of the 15th USAAF had been ordered to raid Zagreb while an impressive force of British and American fighters—Spitfires, Mustangs, Thunderbolts—escorted the trio of flimsy ships.

At 8,000 ft over the Adriatic, then inland from the island of Zirje above snow-covered country towards the Alps, the Russians were hunched dourly in drab greatcoats behind the glider men. General Korneyev guarded two large cases in his baggage. An unsmiling colonel sat near, clutching a tommy-gun. The cases, Turner assumed, were central to this vital flight. It was bitterly cold. Above fir-ridged ravines and white peaks the air became turbulent. Anxiously, they sought the landing zone.

It was a valley named Medenapolu, or Honey Field, slightly north of Bosan Petrovac, the remote winter quarters of the partisans. Casting off about four miles from the target, the glider men swooped across a dazzling landscape, guided by smoke from straw fires lit by the Yugoslavs. The Honey Field was 4,000 ft above sea level; three feet under virgin snow. As the Wacos hit it they stood vertically on their noses before slowly subsiding in the white crust. Immediately, the crews were embraced by 'incredibly filthy and bearded natives' greeting the first Allied planes to land among them since the German occupation.

To the interest of Turner and his fellow pilots, Staff-Sergeants Newman, McCulloch, McMillen, Hill and Morrison, the Russians were suddenly cheerful and avuncular. The colonel with the tommy-gun grinned for the first time. But still Korneyev watched his cases carefully, insisting on travelling with them to Petrovac. There, at a spartan headquarters filled with partisans and the few bedraggled British and American officers who fought with them, the Russians removed their greatcoats to reveal splendid uniforms clustered with decorations. Then they opened the precious chests. They were crammed with vodka and caviare.

It was a useless cargo to desperately impoverished villagers lacking salt, milk, sugar, butter and other basics, as well as arms to repel the Germans when the snows dissolved. But, as Turner saw it, the partisans were duly impressed by Russian affluence. For three hours they ate and drank ceaselessly—the first and only banquet the glider men experienced before the RAF lifted them out when the thaw began.

A few months later the underlying struggle between democracy and communism—a little-publicised flaw in the Alliance—drew crews of the 1st Independent Glider Pilot Squadron to embattled Greece. By October 1944, the German withdrawal from that country had left Athens at the mercy of vicious internal strife as armed political factions fought to gain control. Near Brindisi, at the foot of Italy, British glider pilots prepared a number of old and battered Wacos to fly equipment for paratroops dropping in a race to Athens from nearby Megara, on the Saronic Gulf. Events had turned full circle since Goering's gliders had lifted from Megara to invade Crete.

On 12 October, despite gale winds, men of the 4th Battalion of the 2nd Independent Parachute Brigade dropped on Megara aerodrome. Half the leading company came to grief. Many of the troops, hurled on rocky ground, were stunned and dragged into the gulf by their wind-filled parachutes. The rest secured the field and, as the weather improved, the gliders flew in. The jeeps they carried were valuable. Bereft of transport, much of the sky brigade had to commandeer Greek vehicles to reach the capital. Four months were to pass before peace was restored to Athens.

In Europe, British glider pilots had been involved in two operations outside the main action of their regiment. On 5 August, as preparations for Arnhem were under way, ten Wacos slipped from the dusk over Brittany to land near St

Helene, not far from the port of Lorient. Led by a daring pilot, Captain 'Peggy' Clarke, the flight carried French SAS troops and armed jeeps on a mission to harry Germans and pro-German Russians in the area. Dropping silently, the gliders hit the dusty soil. One crashed in an orchard injuring its fliers, who were left in the care of the local *maquis*. The rest, glider pilots and vengeful SAS men, sped by jeep through darkening lanes to join a group of French freedom fighters at a lakeside farm.

From here the special service men left on sorties, twin Vickers-guns mounted on their vehicles. The glider pilots kept guard on the prisoners sometimes brought in. They were not numerous. The French troops were ruthless, seldom giving and never expecting quarter. One came back from an attack on a pill-box, his shoulder rent by an explosive bullet. Glider pilot John Batley gouged 13 pieces of shrapnel from the man with a knife and dabbed on iodine. There was no anaesthetic. When he had finished, the patient refreshed himself with a crust of bread, replenished his ammunition and left again.

Though discouraged from leaving the farmhouse, the glider pilots occasionally chanced their luck. Staff-Sergeant Bill May and Sergeant Beezum ventured towards Lorient one day. Entering a village, they were warned by its inhabitants that a squad of the enemy had arrived ahead of them. They hid in a cottage until the villagers fetched a guide, an old man with a white beard, to take them back to the *maquis* farm. The Germans, they were told, had offered 20,000 francs for the glider pilots, dead or alive.

The life was harsh. Scrawny steers were slaughtered in the morning and eaten at night with potato whisky and gritty bread. There were no sanitary arrangements. They slept in a rough barn, their prisoners in a pig sty. Some were French. Suspected of working for the Germans, they were treated mercilessly by their compatriots. The glider pilots were reluctant witnesses. 'Feeling sick inside but too scared to say or do anything,' recalled Beezum of a brutal torture incident, 'we crept away to the barn and tried to sleep.'

They were not sorry to learn, some days later, that Allied tanks were approaching nearby Aurai. Beezum was waiting on a corner with his friends when a burly American stopped and asked how long they had been there. Too long, they retorted, demanding to know what had delayed the tanks. The American was not wearing his helmet, and the stars on it eluded them. General Patton took their banter in good part.

The same month, the largest of the independent glider operations was staged against the Germans in southern France. The task was to land men, guns and transport in support of paratroops who would drop in Provence behind the Cote d'Azur. There, amid the palms of Cannes and St Tropez, select enemy troops including many trainee officers, were enjoying a station envied by their comrades fighting to the north.

Their peace was to be interrupted by a hastily assembled American and British division, the First Airborne Task Force, mounted in Italy. Thirty-five Horsas and 40 Wacos, flown by British and Americans, respectively, were to head the glider lift carrying the British 2nd Air Landing Brigade and US 550th Glider Infantry Battalion in the wake of the paratroops. Search parties had discovered some of the Horsas on now-forgotten airstrips in North Africa. Sixteen were found beside a salt lake in the El Djem area. They had been cared for by a party of RAF mechanics forgotten when their squadron had moved on. Other gliders arrived in packing cases, to be assembled on delivery.

The tugs for the operation were C47 Skytrains of the American 54 Troop Carrier Group, a unit with a high reputation among British glider men. The flight, from western Italy across Corsica and the blue Ligurian, was planned to reach France on the morning of 15 August. Glider pilot Major R. Coulthard and his Horsa crews took off from Tarquinia, northwest of Viterbo, before dawn.

Unknown to them, the parachutists were heading for

difficulties. The French Riviera, forsaken that morning by sunshine, lay under thick mist. Though pathfinders dropped safely in the valley of the Argens river, behind the coastal strip, the Eureka beacon they carried proved unreliable, as did receiving equipment with the oncoming fleet. In the leading aircraft the crew chief tried to rectify the fault with a screwdriver, but uncertainty prevailed when they reached France. As a result, paratroops were spread up to 20 miles from their objectives and, while immediate opposition was feeble, they were not able to clear obstacles from all the glider fields.

An hour out on the four-hour flight from Italy, Coulthard's pilots found themselves, to their surprise, hauled through a U-turn and pointed back to Tarquinia. Informed of conditions on the French coast, Brigadier General Paul L. Williams, directing the glider force, had signalled the Horsa tugs to return to base. Two gliders were released over Corsica by tow-planes in trouble. They landed safely on the island. The rest were back in Italy in time for a second breakfast.

Meanwhile the Wacos, which had left slightly later, were flying on. The mist had not cleared when they reached France, and they circled for an hour behind their tugs before they could get down. One had disintegrated in the air, another ditched when its rope broke. Many landed among anti-glider poles, but the guns they carried were soon deployed.

By noon, British paratroops had taken a number of villages near the town of Fréjus, towards the coast, but were missing the equipment from the Horsas which had turned back. At Tarquinia, ground crews were preparing the combinations in frantic haste for another take-off. It was 6 p.m. before Coulthard's men, back in the air after a corned-beef lunch, eventually dived towards French soil. They had spent almost seven hours in their cockpits since reveille. Behind them were 30 artillery pieces, 35 jeeps, nearly 31,400 pounds of ammunition and 233 troops.

Below, the battle now raged for Fréjus. The mist had gone and the wooded slopes of the valley, enfolding vineyards and broken Wacos, drew near with increasing clarity. Then the Horsas were lurching and plunging through poles and other obstacles, winnowing red dust. Coulthard was among the badly injured as they slithered to rest amid vines and trees, but most of the guns were intact, at Fréjus in short time. Backed by later landings of American gliders and more paratroops, the task force achieved its aim.

'It was not,' a British glider pilot recorded phlegmatically, 'one of the spectacular efforts', but the American crews stuck in his memory. 'There is no doubt that the C47 Group was the best that the squadron ever co-operated with, and to them should go the major part of the credit for the success.'

18

Towards the Reckoning

At a time when the Glider Pilot Regiment was shorn of trained men, the RAF had a surplus of flying personnel. RAF Sergeant-Pilot 'Pat' Lewis was one of 46,000 in a reserve pool created by the Empire Training Scheme. Among others, he remembers that the prospect of being transferred to gliders did not hearten them. 'The rumours began after Arnhem and went down badly. Most of the fellows were very positive about the aircraft they hoped to fly. As far as I was concerned, gliders were out of it; I thought Airborne had had it by that time.'

For many, Holland had cast a shadow on the future of the airborne force. General Brereton's own view of his army's capabilities was modified; Browning, leaving to become chief-of-staff in Southeast Asia, doubted if Airborne any longer had a Western role. Britain's 1st Division was shattered, her glider pilot strength halved. The whole employment of the Allied air army was in debate. Within a few months of Arnhem, eight proposals for its use had been shelved, its only action a cross-Channel exercise.

Overall, the value of fighting gliders had not convinced the embattled powers. Hitler had never revived his combat glider force. The few assault operations in which the

Germans used gliders after Crete had been small affairs. Even the most brilliant, the rescue of Mussolini from the Abruzzi mountains by Major Otto Skorzeny and his storm troops, had employed a mere three or four gliders and depended in the end on a powered aircraft. When the Germans used a small gliderborne force in an attempt to seize Tito, the mission failed.

In the East, the Japanese had confined their use of gliders to supply tasks. In 1943 the Hiratsuka factory of the Kokusai Koku Aircraft Company had begun production of a small transport glider, the Gander, capable of carrying 18 equipped troops or a light gun. Towed by the Mitsubishi heavy bomber, the Gander was of curious origin, having evolved from a twin-engined aeroplane with its motors displaced. Significantly, the best of the larger Japanese gliders, a twin-boomed aircraft, the Ku-7, was eventually produced as a powered plane, like the German Giant. Ganders turned up in the Philippines; the Ku-7 was not used operationally.

Despite Wingate's lead, the East never became a major war glider zone. In India, recruiting and training had gone forward, but problems were manifold. Wooden planes tended to warp in the humid atmosphere, transport from England was difficult, the cost of building gliders on the spot proved prohibitive. Moreover, four-engined aircraft, essential for lifting Horsas in the climate, were scarce in India. Plans there would at length be overtaken by the atom bomb.

In Britain, Brereton's staff was still pondering when, in mid-December, the Germans launched a violent and unexpected offensive in the Ardennes. Headed by panzer units using American equipment to spread confusion, three German armies smashed west towards the Meuse. By 19 December their penetration was so deep as to impair General Omar N. Bradley's communications, and Eisenhower had halted Allied advances elsewhere. Suddenly, generals were calling for airborne formations to stem the tide as ground troops. Both American air divisions were trucked forward, the 101st to hold surrounded Bastogne for five days. The

British 1st was still out of action, the 6th fighting to the north as infantry. There seemed, indeed, little scope for further airborne schemes.

But Sergeant-Pilot Lewis's outlook was premature. For more than a month Allied operations were delayed while the German attack was contained and repulsed, then Eisenhower looked to the Rhine again. This time his eye fell on a stretch of the river southeast of Arnhem, near Wesel, an important traffic centre above the Ruhr. There was to be no dependence on a single bridge. Instead, the plan was to force the river on a 20-mile front in the biggest amphibious operation since Normandy.

The directive, issued from Montgomery's headquarters on 9 March, 1945, defined his intention 'to cross the Rhine north of the Ruhr and secure a firm bridgehead with a view to developing operations to isolate the Ruhr and to penetrate deeper into Germany'. In brief, the general plan was:

> To cross the Rhine on a front of two armies . . . Ninth Army (American) being on the right and Second Army (British) on the left.
>
> To capture the communication centre of Wesel.
>
> To expand the initial lodgement area on the east bank of the Rhine:
>
> (a) southwards for a sufficient distance to secure the road centre of Wesel from enemy ground action.
>
> (b) northwards to enable the river to be bridged at Emmerich and the road centre at that place to be used.
>
> (c) eastwards and northeast in order to secure rapidly a good and firm bridgehead from which further offensive operations can suitably be developed.
>
> To position the three armies of 21 Army Group east of the Rhine, and north of the Ruhr, so that further operations deeper into Germany can be developed quickly in any direction as may be ordered by Supreme HQ.

Against the run of speculation in many quarters, the operation called for the largest airborne lift ever made.

The British glider chief, with more than 500 men on his casualty list and, unlike the RAF, no reserves, was faced with the onerous responsibility of bringing his glider force to full strength in short time. Though it confounded his doctrine that glider pilots should be first-class fighting soldiers, his only recourse was to obtain trained pilots from the RAF. To his frustration, the Air Ministry at first refused to think of it. Incensed, Chatterton appealed to the RAF's director of training, Air Chief Marshal Sir Peter Drummond. With Drummond's approval, 1,500 pilots were provided by the RAF.

Sergeant-Pilot Lewis saw many of his companions go. 'Quite a few felt pretty mutinous. They'd volunteered for the RAF and saw this as an army job. To their mind, gliders were boxes with wings on them. They had no desire to be pitched into battle like infantrymen. Most, however, accepted the necessity. I met some afterwards—they had caught the spirit of the glider boys.'

The majority, converting on Hotspurs, were given Horsas to fly on the operation. Some, among them Flying Officer John Love and Sergeant-Pilot McEwan, got Hamilcars. Sitting above a Tetrarch tank in the massive and powerless aircraft was a novel experience for the air force men. With the veterans of Arnhem, they now studied the latest plans.

Mass landings, as in Holland, were under question. Not only were the Germans familiar with the method, they were known to have devised counter-measures. As they recognised, glider forces unloading and assembling at the point of a massed landing were vulnerable to interruption by relatively small numbers of determined troops. Special mobile units had been raised by the Germans to rush to the scene of airborne landings, directed by an alarm system operated by all commands. The philosophy was embodied in a report by Major Sepp Krafft, whose small unit had delayed Urquhart's first thrust at Arnhem.

'It is vitally important to attack the enemy immediately with all forces available, not with any hope of destroying him but to disturb and disrupt his preparations for battle . . . pin him down to secure time to prepare counter-measures.'

Krafft stressed the importance of engaging gliders with small-arms. 'The gliders are most vulnerable between casting off and landing. . . . For a long time standing orders of the German army have been that enemy aircraft will be attacked with all infantry weapons. How much more important is this in the case of gliders, larger and slower targets. It has been found on examination that nearly every shot gets home. The gliders [at Arnhem] were holed by countless hits and the bloodstains inside showed that the enemy had suffered appreciable casualties in the air.'

To offset German preparedness for mass landings, and meet the demand of troop commanders to be put down close to their objectives, Chatterton advocated and rehearsed a 'tactical' landing plan whereby each glider, or group of gliders, disgorged its occupants as near as possible to where they needed to be in the battle scheme. It meant the methodical streaming of gliders according to the units they carried, and the maintainance of sequence on the fly-in. At the same time, the interval between release and touch-down was to be kept short. The new technique was adopted for the assault.

And there were new—or rather, modified—aircraft, too. Despite the introduction of quick-release nuts, explosive surcingles and other devices, the Horsa had continued to present unloading problems. Difficulties met at Normandy had been experienced again at Arnhem, crews still struggling in some cases with saws and wire-cutters to remove the tail sections. Nor was loading as easy as it might be, the insertion of guns and vehicles through the door aft the cockpit involving a ninety-degrees turn at the top of a steep ramp. To ease matters, the Mark II Horsas now in service had been designed with a hinged nose, the pilots' cabin swinging aside to provide straight in-and-out cargo movement.

Prudently, the rear unloading system was retained in case the nose jammed on landing, the extra option considerably reducing the risk of delay in action. The improved Horsa also carried extra load. In lieu of 28 fully equipped troops, it could lift two 5-cwt vehicles, or one vehicle and 75 mm howitzer with crew and ammunition, the weight exceeding that of the Mark I by 250 pounds.

Changes in tactics and equipment struck a timely note, for as Lawrence Wright of the RAF planning unit (now ensconced in 'a crumbling Jacobean pile' near Chatterton's headquarters) described the scheme for the Wesel crossing, its use of the airborne army was 'highly unorthodox'. It would not, as usual, go into action before the ground forces, but after the river assault commenced, dropping just ahead of the advanced formations on the battlefield. 'Small friendly units,' it was hinted uncertainly, 'may be in the vicinity of the landing zones.'

Little else in the plan could be termed small. Night after night, as the day drew near, troops and equipment moved towards the assault sector in the kind of invasion build-up not seen since D-Day. Rehabilitated Dutch and Belgian road maintenance departments had worked feverishly with seven battalions of American assault engineers, and British sappers and pioneers, to accommodate the traffic streams. Among the mass of equipment entailed were 4,000 tank transporters and 32,000 other vehicles. Amphibious tanks and Buffalo troop carriers waited with the leading assault forces, two corps of the British Second Army and a corps of the United States Ninth Army. Thirty-six naval landing craft, hauled forward on 24-wheeler trailers, were ready to be launched. Convoys of lorries bore pontoons and bridging elements.

Before the attack, the Second Army would have brought up 118,000 tons of ammunition, petrol and other stores; the Ninth Army, 138,000 tons.

For days the resources of the Allied air forces were carefully directed to isolate the Wesel region from the Ruhr and pound enemy defences, barracks and airfields. It was known that the far bank of the Rhine was held by some of the best divisions left to the Germans, with a strong allotment of tanks and self-propelled guns. Especially fierce resistance was expected from three divisions of the German 2nd Parachute Corps, and the 47th Panzer Corps in reserve.

The most important defence feature on the German bank was an area of high wooded ground straggling northwest of Wesel and known as the Diersfordter Wald. Apart from this, the Rhine plain in the sector was flat and rather featureless, so that the Diersfordter Wald not only dominated the river and its immediate flats to the west but provided a natural protective ridge in front of a lesser river to the east, the Issel, the Issel bridges, and the small town of Hamminkeln beside a road junction and railway line. This vital area, including the heights, was to be the objective of the airborne army.

The air armada, comprising 1,600 powered aircraft and more than 1,300 gliders—the Americans would use their customary double-tow technique—was to lift some 17,000 glider troops and parachutists of the British 6th and the US 17th Airborne Divisions, together with tons of supplies, armour and other equipment. About 860 of the gliders would be Wacos, 440 Horsas and 48 Hamilcars. The British division was to take the northern part of the Diersfordter Wald, Hamminkeln and two of the Issel bridges; the American division, the southern part of the wood and the Issel bridges to the east of it.

Unlike 'Market Garden', with its three-day spread of drops, the whole airborne operation at Wesel, coded 'Varsity', would go down in four hours, including the re-supply drop.

The force could not expect to surprise the enemy. The Germans would be alerted by the river assault, but the drop would divert forces from those opposing the crossing, obliging them to fight two battles at once. The consequences for the glider men remained to be discovered. The veterans of Arnhem had few illusions—it would be a bloody reckoning. For the RAF pilots switched to gliders, the prospect of landing in the heat of a battle raised urgent doubts. Their experience as soldiers amounted, in many cases, to a training course of three weeks.

19

The Rhine Again

On the morning of 24 March, 1945, Lieutenant Sydney St John, 'the old man of the regiment', as he recalls it, flew to battle for the first time in his army career. At 32, slim and amiable, he had passed much of his service on coastal defence batteries before volunteering to fly gliders as a means of joining the 'fighting war'. When his age had raised eyebrows, St John, a Conservative party organiser in civilian life, had 'used my committee experience with the selection board'. Now he wondered what landing on the battlefield would be like.

Another greener, Sergeant-Pilot Bill McFayden of the RAF, was sure of one thing—'If I met a six-foot German with a bayonet when I landed, the odds were on the German. I'd never expected to fight on the ground when I joined the RAF, and a bit of hasty training hadn't taught me much.' McFayden, 21 years old, was flying a Horsa with his fellow Scot, Andrew McGregor, an older man with the rank of flying officer. They had named their glider 'The Wee McGregor Patrol', but McGregor had been unusually serious as the day approached.

The nearness of victory gave danger a special edge. The more experienced the pilots, it seemed to St John, the more tense they were. He had noticed that Staff-Sergeant Harrison, a versed campaigner, was apprehensive; that Captain Rex Norton, another veteran, had sat up writing letters until late at night. On the airfields of eastern England many Arnhem survivors nursed anxieties. So did the glider pilots from America, now in France.

For some, observed writer Milton Dank, who was one of them, there was a strong need to be alone; 'in solitude they studied the photographs of the landing fields, as if to discover in the lacework of lines or in the various greyish tints the fate which awaited them.' Others walked in the gloom that morning, 'around and around the inside perimeter of the airfield until it began to get light'. Clifford Tuppen, a British glider pilot, had slept fitfully, awake before reveille with the details of his briefing on his mind. Tuppen had memorised 'every tree and field, and the concentration of German artillery'.

Reveille for the British airborne troops was at 2.45 a.m. Ninety minutes later, after breakfast in 'blacked out' messes, parachutists and glider soldiers were heading for the airfields in jolting lorries. On dark aerodromes they donned life-jackets and parachutes, and were issued with the tablets alleged to prevent air-sickness. The paratroops of the 3rd and 5th Brigades were to be carried by planes of the US Air Force; the 6th Air Landing Brigade in Horsas and Hamilcars towed by the RAF. It was light as they climbed aboard.

St John's Horsa took a jeep, a motor-cycle and a dozen men. The sky, as they rose behind the Halifax, was bright and clear. There was a morning haze but no cloud, and the sou'southeasterly wind was light. The British gliders were lifting from eight fields. At one, Gosfield, the Horsas carrying the bridge-assault parties were airborne by seven o'clock. At Earls Colne 30 gliders took off in as many minutes. Elsewhere, a tow-plane crashed but the glider, unharmed, was found another tug.

At Woodbridge, the Hamilcar base in Essex, 48 great gliders were hauled aloft in under half an hour. Flying Officer

John Love of the RAF took off smoothly. Love, a volunteer to fly gliders, had thrown himself conscientiously into the fortnight of small-arms instruction and week of field training that qualified him as an 'honorary' soldier. He was glad his glider was a Hamilcar. True, it was the most inviting of all targets for anti-aircraft fire; its 36,000 lbs loaded took some landing, and if it tipped on its back the cargo fell on the pilots. For all that, Love thought the squadron a 'plum posting'.

The British gliders assembled over Hawkinge, Kent. It was, St John remembers, an amazing sight. Hundreds of aircraft were converging in streams which stretched as far as the eye could see, forming three great lanes towards the Continent. 'Visibility was perfect and everywhere you looked there were tugs and gliders. It was extraordinary.' Seasoned glider campaigners were no less impressed. Boucher-Giles recalled the thrill of spotting the crowds which gathered in towns to stare up at them.

The usual scattering of machines in trouble was under way. Ten gliders went down in England, ropes broken or tugs in difficulty, and two ditched in the Channel, where launches were standing by. More than 420 crossed the French coast. Riding east, the force contained the largest number of glider pilots Iain Murray had commanded on a single lift. The colonel recalls a personally smooth, uneventful flight, though others remember a rougher time. Where planes had passed, the air was choppy and some Horsas (notably the Mark IIs) tended to roll excessively. Nineteen gliders went down between the French coast and the Rhine. One, a Hamilcar, disintegrated in the air, its tank and all aboard hurled to earth.

St John had to struggle for control in the centre stream, where his Australian-crewed tug had positioned him. In 'The Wee McGregor Patrol' the pilots flew in turn. For McFayden the four-hour flight culminated a week of briefings and pep-talks that made his head reel. Finally, a brigadier had stood up and told them breezily: 'Won't those blighters be amazed when we cross the Rhine!' McFayden took heart from it.

Anyone, he thought, would be amazed to see 1,300 gliders coming down on them.

Glider pilot Page, who had flown to Arnhem in sanguine mood, was to land beside one of the Issel bridges. Neither he nor the assault troops he carried were complacent this time. Staff-Sergeant Shingleton, after his lucky escape across the river, was returning to the Rhine with men and equipment for a field ambulance. Airborne doctors and their teams were prepared to deal with heavy casualties. The commander of 224th (parachute) Field Ambulance, warned to expect up to 600 cases in the 3rd Brigade, had attached an MO and staff of 16 with each battalion. All members of his headquarters carried bottles of plasma on them, while pre-sterilised surgical instruments—then an innovation—were on the aircraft.

Murray knew that the landings would be dangerous. He also knew they were vital to the advance. 'It was quite obvious that unless we secured the Diersfordter Wald the main operation would be threatened from the high ground. Germans there could inflict appalling injury on our forces on the plain below.'

Colonel Charles H. Young, an American glider commander, had told his pilots that what they were about to do would contribute 'to the rapid ending of the war'. Much had been done to diminish the opposition. In two days, ten Luftwaffe airfields had received more than 2,700 tons of bombs from Allied aircraft, 168 enemy planes had been destroyed and flak positions had been bombed and rocketed. Nevertheless, American pilots were reminded, the Germans would be alert and on their homeland. It was not Holland. There would be no friendly civilians.

The first of the US paratroop transports left Chartres with the 507th Parachute Regiment as the British fleet climbed east. Other troop planes of the 17th Division lifted from fields in the Paris region, followed by the glider fleet. Double-tow take-offs were not helped in some cases by a crosswind. Wacos fouled the ropes of their tow ships. Two had their wings sheered off and crashed. But most rose safely and, by 8 a.m., were streaming towards Belgium and the British train.

In almost perfect weather, the two fleets met side by side over Wavre, near Brussels, and the greatest glider armada of the war was formed. American glider pilot Paul C. Swink had time to survey the concourse. It was the first mission he had flown with a second pilot, and Flight Officer Swink enjoyed the luxury of relaxing while another worked. Staff-Sergeant Miller, in his Horsa, felt a sense of pride. Miller could imagine the satisfaction of the Belgians who gazed up at them. For five years Europe had bowed to the Nazi yoke. Now its liberated citizens saw an army in the sky bound for Germany. 'It made you feel good to be a part of it.'

The responsibility of General Wilhelm Schlemm was unenviable. That month he had been ordered to defend the Wesel sector. The German armies were depleted, some units demoralised. Of those to the east of the Rhine, many had taken a beating on the west bank due to Hitler's refusal to countenance withdrawal while they were in better shape. On 10 March, the Führer had sacrificed Field Marshal Gerd von Rundstedt, his western commander, as a scapegoat for the defeats of the past months. It was Rundstedt's successor, Field Marshal Albert von Kesselring, who had given General Schlemm the Wesel front.

Schlemm knew there was little time—in fact, less than two weeks—before the Allies assaulted the river there. The mainstay of his force, the tough First Parachute Army, was seriously short of men and material; his 86th Corps of patchy quality. At the general's insistence he was allocated the high-grade 57th Panzer Corps for extra punch. This he held in reserve to the north, his front above Wesel comprising mainly paratroops; that to the south, mainly infantry.

Half-tracks and lorries hauled guns to the Diersfordter Wald. From its dominating perches, artillery covered the plain below. The forest was thick with hidden batteries.

Troops moved into houses, sandbagging windows and digging trenches. Every farm became an army post. Schlemm knew that airborne attack was almost certain, but did not know where it might materialise. There was no time to put up anti-glider poles. The planes would have to be hit as they came down, and guns abounded for this purpose, well camouflaged. Indeed, Schlemm's anti-aircraft defences were seriously underestimated by the Allies.

Through March, German commanders trained their field-glasses to the west. Expecting sky troops to lead the action, they were puzzled by their absence when the move began. At nine o'cock on the night of the 23rd, the British 51st (Highland) Division, with a brigade of Canadians, made for the river bank. Sloshing through flood water, 150 Buffaloes entered the stream and swam across, soon followed by craft along the whole front. Some landed without trouble. Elsewhere, mud sucked at the amphibious vehicles, swimming tanks floundered, troop-carriers were thwarted by stone-pitched shores.

Succeeding waves of the attack found much of the bank still in German hands. To the north, part of the 51st was cut off at a village named Speldrop by German paratroops. At Wesel the Commandos, entering what was left after a devastating bomber raid, tackled defenders while the Americans advanced to the right of them. Next morning, as the mists of the Westphalian plain rose, the battle was engaged across 20 miles.

On a hill near Xanten, a town on the west bank, a distinguished group watched developments. Winston Churchill had flown to Montgomery's headquarters to witness the operation with his chief of staff, Field Marshal Alan Brooke. Among those beside them, as history unfolded across the stream, were Eisenhower and Brereton. Through the haze, they could just make out the curve of the Rhine as it stretched towards Wesel in front of the Diersfordter Wald. Around them, the noise of Allied artillery was thunderous, more than 3,000 guns supporting the attacking troops.

Then, suddenly, the firing ended and the air was quiet. To the rear, above Weeze, west of Xanten, the sound of engines grew. Eyes turned skyward. The volume rose and the van of the air army came in sight.

Wrote Churchill afterwards: 'It was full daylight before the subdued but intense roar and rumbling of swarms of aircraft stole upon us. After that, in the course of half an hour, over two thousand aircraft streamed overhead in their formation. My viewpoint was well chosen. The light was clear enough to enable me to see where the descent on the enemy took place. The aircraft faded from sight . . . but now there was a double murmur and roar of reinforcements. . . . Soon one saw with a sense of tragedy aircraft in twos and threes coming back askew, asmoke or even in flames.'

What the prime minister could not see was the extraordinary air pollution above the landing zone, a stratum of murk described by a reporter in a Halifax as 'a gigantic curtain over the battlefield, hiding all that was going on underneath'. Vic Miller, flying a Horsa, remembers the green light signalling him to release from his Stirling tug and being unable to pick out anything on the ground. 'I hung on hoping for a gap, a glimpse of something. It was a total blank.'

St John, like most pilots, was nonplussed by the great cloud. No warning had been given of the phenomenon and he pondered its proportions with trepidation. Some fliers, remembering Merville, attributed it to shelling or bomb attacks. Brigadier G. K. Bourne, a British airborne commander, first observed it from a glider above the Meuse. 'From there I could see the Rhine, a silver streak, and beyond it a thick black haze, for all the world like Manchester or Birmingham as seen from the air. For the moment, I wondered whether the bombing of Wesel, which had preceded the attack upon that town by Commando troops, had been mis-timed. If this was so, then the whole landing zone would be obscured by the clouds of dust which would be blowing from the rubble created by the attack.'

Major Hugh J. Nevins of Kansas City, flying the first Waco to cross the Rhine, blamed smoke generators for the hazard. Nevins became aware of the manifestation as he and co-pilot Lieutenant Bob Burke approached the river. 'It was here that Bob and I first saw Marshal Montgomery's unannounced smokescreen at Wesel, billowing northeast to cover the movement of his troops across the river. Unfortunately, the smokescreen was cloud-like, and in penetrating it we encountered horizontal visibilities as low as one-quarter of a mile.'

Other pilots, reporting German smoke-cannisters, later claimed that the cloud was an anti-airborne ploy by the enemy. The truth contained something of all theories, conditions contriving to assemble the smoke, dust and fumes of battle in one huge canopy. 'It reminded me,' said one pilot, 'of a passage by Walter Scott: *at weapon point they close. They close, in clouds of smoke and dust.* . . . Whatever caused it, it was formidable, and there was no avoiding it.'

In a moment, gliders would be descending on all sides. That they should be forced to do so through a layer of blinding murk stretching almost to the ground from several hundred feet was as daunting as it was unforeseen. Murray recalls being 'more apprehensive about the smoke than anything. At first it hid us from the German gunners on the ground, but I wondered if the pilots could find their landing places—and, if not, what would become of them.'

20

Battlefield

Miller searched for a hole in the smoke and dust. Combinations were bunching above the battlefield, some climbing to avoid those ahead. His own tug had flown in at 2,000 ft. Others were 1,000 ft higher, and he could see Halifaxes on a reciprocal course below, their gliders gone. Flak was bursting. Miller saw a Halifax catch fire, white silks spreading as its crew jumped. It was a sudden and unpleasant reminder that neither glider pilots nor their passengers had parachutes.

He had delayed his release as long as possible. Now he cut and went down through the rending shells. Behind him, as in hundreds of gliders, the troops were tense. In Boucher-Giles's Horsa a sergeant-major of the Devons told him he was not bothered about the battle: 'It's this landing that worries me.' Brigadier Bourne had fixed his straps and, as his glider went into a steep dive, strained to catch the anxious conversation of the pilots. It was the first operation for both of them.

'Now,' advised the sergeant beside Howard Cowan, a war reporter, 'is when you pray.' Blood was already streaming down the face of a trooper in Cowan's Waco. The man's head had hit the framework of the glider before release. There was another lurch as the pilot banked and smoke from the cloud filled the fuselage, thick and acrid, 'like being in a burning house'.

Suddenly, Miller could see the ground. The fumes had parted and through the gap he made out an autobahn near the Issal which he knew from the landing maps. Then the gap closed. His second pilot was an RAF sergeant named Gordon. Miller recalls turning to Gordon in the blinding smoke. 'For God's sake,' he shouted, 'if you see a space with gliders on it, we'll have a go.' He had given up hope of finding their assigned zone. They emerged from the murk above farmland. 'I couldn't believe my eyes. I was looking at the very field we had been briefed to put our soldiers in.'

St John had released at 1,500 ft and completed more than half his descent when he entered smoke. Horrified, he had watched the glider ahead of him catch fire, then 'I couldn't see a thing and was too concerned with my own difficulties to dwell on others'. He came out of the cloud at treetop level, buried the glider in the soft ground and clambered out as bullets flew. Only one of his passengers had been knocked out. The rest lay on their faces beneath a wing, wondering how to unload the bunkered plane.

Miller's relief at finding his landing field was short-lived. Descending almost vertically with full flap, he found himself looking down at German soldiers. They were in a farmyard, firing up at him. Another glider had crashed into the farmhouse. Its tail was sticking out of the broken roof. Levelling the Horsa, he skimmed the field, aware he was not going to stop in time. He was approaching two poles which carried power-cables beside a road. Another glider, Clifford Tuppen's, had just scraped a line of cables as it landed. They had cut the bottom from the cockpit like cheese wire slicing Parmesan. Miller opted to fly beneath the strung wires.

As he did so, the Horsa touched the road, bounced, lost a wing-tip on a pole, and settled on ploughed land. Shots slammed into the glider as the troops debarked. Few had time to give thanks for delivery. Reporter Cowan heard someone shouting 'Get out of here!' and was crawling next moment towards a ditch while bullets tore divots from the moist turf. Rolling into a foot of slimy water, he was tempted to drink it to slake his parched throat.

Gliders were landing at mad speeds. Murray, down safely, watched a Horsa crash. 'It must have been doing 150 miles an hour,' he remembers. 'The fire from the ground was so intense that many pilots, especially the RAF men, were tempted to land too fast. You could hardly blame them. The majority of gliders were being struck as they came down.'

Glider pilot Andrews had no flaps to control his speed. Several shells had burst close as he descended. His second pilot had been hit, shrapnel had hammered the jeep they carried. Now, as Andrews tried first half-flap then full-flap, nothing happened save that the controls got heavy and the rate of descent increased alarmingly. Fighting for response, he skimmed a line of poplar trees, clipped the vertical wing of a crashed plane and cartwheeled. Staff-Sergeant Andrews was hurled clear. Looking up, he saw that the entire front of the glider had gone, the wings had collapsed and the tail had broken off.

Groggily, he began to pull others from the wreckage. They were in a heap under the wings, men on top of each other, pieces of seat and seating harness still strapped to them. Three were missing. Andrews never discovered what became of them.

McFayden's glider also lost flap control. As 'the Wee McGregor Patrol' approached the ground it was clear they were going to overshoot. A wood was looming. Desperately, they steered for an opening between the trees. McFayden recalls missing the first of them, then the crash. Flung through the nose, he lost consciousness. When he came to, he found the jeep on top of him. 'As we came down, I'd put on my steel helmet. Now one side of the rim was in the ground, the other side wedged under the vehicle. In between was my head. Only the helmet was keeping it from being crushed.'

Coughing dirt from his mouth, the young RAF sergeant

called for help. He was rescued by some paratroops. McGregor had been killed, as had the sergeant in charge of the jeep crew. Lingering by the wreck in a state of shock, McFayden looked up to see a soldier coming through the trees. It was the brigadier who had addressed them the night before. 'It seemed like a dream. He looked at my injured foot and said, "How are you, sonny? Don't worry. You'll soon be back across the Rhine".'

Visibility was 'almost nil' as Captain Boucher-Giles's bullet-peppered glider winged to the east of the Diersfordter Wald. Sliding from the smoke, it ploughed into a field and immediately came under fire again. There were only seven men aboard but most had automatic weapons. They blazed back at the Germans until things quietened, then decided to unload. The Horsa was the old type. For some reason, nobody had the key to unlock the tail.

After some hectic but futile slashing at wires with the axe they carried, they got out the explosive cord. The pilots were fixing it when a fresh burst of fire swept the small group. All but two were killed or wounded—the sergeant-major who had worried about the landing, among the dead. Boucher-Giles felt a blow high on the thigh. He came round after passing out to find that his second pilot, Sergeant Garland, had scraped a trench in the ploughland, pulled him into it and dressed the wound.

Lieutenant St John had sprawled by his glider half an hour, wondering how to remove the jeep. 'In the end, we blew the tail off with a hand-grenade. The jeep was undamaged and its crew got away on it.' Apprehensively, St John approached a farmhouse. He was confronted there by an imperturbable German matron, the first enemy he had met face to face. 'She put a plate of steak and chips in front of me. I suppose stranger things have happened on battlefields, but I certainly hadn't expected a cooked meal. We were lads and she fussed like anybody's mum might.'

Crouched in a shell-hole, Miller was taking cover as shots flew from a German post in some farm buildings. Nearby, a

Horsa had crashed killing his comrade, Staff-Sergeant George Duns, and the co-pilot. No one was alive in it. Miller swung his rifle as a man approached. The soldier stood on the lip of the hole, a bazooka pointing down. 'I would have fired but I saw his shoulder-flash just in time. He was American. I couldn't make out what he was doing there. I told him to point his bazooka elsewhere.'

Grunting, the American fired it at the buildings, surveyed the damage and strolled away. As Miller advanced, he saw more Americans. One was hanging dead in the straps of his parachute. Another lay in a furrow, covered with blood. His mouth was open, full of soil, as if he had been shouting when he hit the earth. Several more, killed by machine-gun fire, lay not far away. 'I began to wonder what was happening. The Americans should have been to the south of us. I looked up at the cloud of smoke and saw a Waco come out of it at a frightening speed. The troops had stuck their guns through the canvas sides and were firing crazily. It passed from sight and I heard the crash.'

The first paratroop transports had approached the Diersfordter Wald in a calm sky. There was no flak and the navigators were better equipped to estimate target zones through the cloud than were glider pilots. They dropped the British 3rd Parachute Brigade accurately on the northwest side of the forest, the 5th Brigade nearer Hamminkeln, on the northeast. Then the blast began. As the aircraft turned for home, sweeping outside the layer of dust and smoke, Schlemm's anti-aircraft batteries ravaged them. The transports burned easily. Ten dropped east of the Rhine within minutes; others, streaming fire, held course to crash on the west bank.

At the same time, the German troops took aim at the drifting parachutists. Many were killed as they landed, including the commander of a Canadian battalion which was badly hit. Others entangled in the high trees. Parachute padre the Rev. Kenny was killed as he swung helplessly. So were

Driver Shelton and Corporal Nicholson of the same brigade. Sergeant Slater drew a knife and slashed his lift-webbs. A physical training instructor, Slater fell 20 ft but was unharmed. Captain Anderson, quartermaster of a medical unit, was brought to earth when a mortar bomb struck the tree which had fouled him. Amazingly, Anderson was not hurt. Moments later he was shot as he went to the aid of a wounded trooper.

Elsewhere, American paratroops were floating down. Many of their transports had missed the mark. Seventy-two C46s, flown from France, dropped the 513th Parachute Infantry and the 466th Parachute Field Artillery Battalion in the British sector. Some fell where gliders were due to land, and helped to clear the zone. Strongly opposed, they fought fiercely, sustaining a lot of casualties.

Soon, airborne medical units were working non-stop. At one post, manned by staff of 244th Field Ambulance in a battered church, the flow of wounded was continuous. Soldiers of both sides lay injured beside civilians. One man had ten pounds of metal in his pelvis; an ageing civilian, found with his abdomen gaping, died under morphia. At first, parachuted medical staff coped alone. Reinforcement by glider was imperative.

Staff-Sergeant Shingleton landed his Horsa, with field ambulance passengers, in good shape. Jumping out, the glider pilots discovered themselves between a line of advancing Americans and the Germans holding a nearby wood. Unloading was delayed while the two fought. Meanwhile, another glider carrying medical equipment struck the top of the forest, its pilot killed.

One of the immediate casualties picked up by 3 Section of the gliderborne 195th Field Ambulance was an American paratrooper with a broken leg. Under mortar and small-arms fire, the section travelled more than a mile to divisional headquarters at Kopenhof Farm, south of Hamminkeln, to find its casualty post in the hands of a frantic German doctor and his orderlies. The flow of wounded was incessant, landing brigade casualties then reckoned at 40 per cent. The British MO took over. Soon every room at his disposal was jampacked.

Still the gliders swirled to the battlefield. 'They were like locusts,' reported a German gunner; 'you hit one and half a dozen took its place. Everybody was shooting, but they kept coming. Some must have flown themselves, for no one could have lived in them.' Glider pilot Reynolds, an RAF squadron leader, was engaged the whole way down by a four-pit anti-aircraft battery in a railway yard. The port wheel of his Horsa was shot off. As the glider approached the gun pits, its second pilot stood up in the cockpit firing a sten through the vision panel. The troops Reynolds landed took the battery.

Anti-aircraft fire struck Love's Hamilcar as he began his descent, and his legs were hit. Seconds later, the big ship was caught again. It sank through the smoke shedding pieces, hydraulics smashed, moiled agonisingly across a field and put its massive nose in a ditch. Unable to release the tank, the men in the hull scrambled out, joined by McEwan, the second pilot. Love's legs were jammed. He called down that he would stay put. Almost simultaneously, a German machine-gun sprayed the cockpit. Love was suddenly in the ditch, waist-deep in water, despite his legs.

With Love and the army subaltern from the glider wounded, Sergeant-Pilot McEwan, fortified by three weeks army training, took command of the glider troops.

Pilots Jenkins and Anderson had watched a nearby ship fall on fire, portions breaking from its fuselage. Now, like others, they were lost above the smoke, only their compass to guide the flight. They went down in ninety-degree turns, losing 200 ft on each leg, to avoid drifting from the zone. Though Anderson stood up to maximise his field of vision, they completed the box without sighting ground. Then, ahead and slightly starboard, they glimpsed an opening. It was circular, about the size of a sunflower as they saw it, and held in perfect miniature a church spire.

Jenkins turned over it at 600 ft, put on full flap and went down. Later, he remembered how the stones in the cemetery stood out. Clipping a tree, they pitched into a field and dived from the glider to furrowed earth. Two soldiers were shot as they did so. The stones, Jenkins remembered, had been stark and white.

As Harry Antonopoulos started to leave his Horsa it was hit by automatic fire. The burst was so rapid the bullets came through one hole. Diving clear, glider pilot Antonopoulos was seeking cover when a voice called, 'Over here, buddy'. He joined several Americans in a ditch. Reporter Cowan had slithered out of his own ditch. Cowan had grown cold in the water, and the shooting thereabouts had quietened. For an anxious moment, he imagined a glider would crash on him. It had sheered the top from a tree close by, but landed a hundred yards away. His wounded companions received aid. One had a bullet through the top of his skull. It had gone into his helmet and out again, yet the man was conscious as they dressed the wound.

Heroic efforts were made to get the wounded from the landing fields. When British medical orderlies Lenton and Downey proposed crossing open ground to the gliders, their section leader told them, 'You'll never get there and back alive'. They did—bringing not only the wounded but a supply of much-needed stretchers from the aircraft.

At about 11 a.m., cries for help from a maimed glider man drew two orderlies from 224th Field Ambulance to open ground. Both were killed as they knelt over him. Corporal Topham, a Canadian 'medic', had seen them shot. Scrambling forward, he began in turn to work on the wounded man. As he did so, a bullet went through his nose. Despite the blood and intense pain, Topham completed first-aid on the soldier before carrying him to safety through continuing fire. For two hours the Canadian ignored his own wound, repeatedly rescuing glider men.

Sound or injured, alive or dead, more than 800 British glider pilots reached the battlefield. Some were celebrated for their good luck. Staff-Sergeant Nigel Brown upheld his reputation for a charmed life by touching down perfectly. According to squadron legend, Brown stepped from his Horsa adjusting a silk scarf and equally unruffled when the heavy machine-gun of a German tank shot a bren-gun out of his hands. 'Actually,' Brown recalls, 'it was two tanks, but I wasn't holding the bren when it was hit. I'd stepped behind a tree for a moment. It shielded me.'

Others were cast in bizarre tragedies. One pilot, thrown clear of his smashed glider, found his rifle almost bent in halves. Every passenger was dead or grimly injured. Dazedly, he shuffled back to the debris and rested on a wheel. He was still sitting there, head in hands, rifle useless, when a squad of Germans appeared and surrendered to him.

2 1

'Hiya, Bud!'

While the gliders dropped beyond the Diersfordt Wald, assaults by river mounted against the German front. The British 15th Division punched for the woods themselves, aiming to link with 6th Airborne; the 51st was still grimly engaged to the left, where its commander, Major-General T. G. Rennie, was killed that morning. Here, German parachute divisions, reinforced by the 15th Panzer Grenadier Division, continued to pin part of the attacking force at Speldrop, fiercely contesting the thrust east. Holding at Rees, on the river south of Speldrop, Schlemm's 8th Parachute Division, supported by artillery, swept the river with daunting fire.

At Wesel, Commandos had attacked the German head-quarters soon after dawn, killing its commander and securing the position. To their right, men of the US 30th Division were striking east parallel with the River Lippe, which joined the Rhine at Wesel, while their compatriots of the 79th Division thrust for Dinslaken, a road and rail junction three miles beyond the main stream. At several points on the river, engineers were fighting the swollen current to establish bridges by which the Allies might reinforce their forward troops.

Overhead, a special force of gliders had winged towards

the Issel, behind Schlemm's front, to seize other bridges
before German reinforcements could cross by them.

The glider pilots, and the troops they carried, had trained
carefully. Staff-Sergeant Page, flying a Horsa to the
northernmost of the road bridges, had been rehearsed for
several weeks in England. His glider was one of three
assigned to land on the east side of the bridge, farthest from
the main landings, while five others took the west side.
Page's task was to place his Horsa with a wing actually across
the deep-cut waterway to provide an escape for the assault
troops should they find themselves trapped on the far bank.

According to Allied intelligence, 200 German paratroops
had moved into dwellings around the bridge. Each of the
three gliders for the east bank carried 26 men of the Ox. and
Bucks. Light Infantry. The flight, under glider pilot Captain
A. M. D. Carr, left Gosfield, Essex, in the van of the glider
fleet, passing over the main landing zones beyond the Rhine
towards Ringenberg, a small town east of Hamminkeln. The
smoke of battle was now behind and the Issel came in view.
The gliders cut free.

Page recalls releasing at 2,500 ft. Ahead, the other two
gliders, led by Carr, began their descent. As they did so an
88 mm anti-aircraft gun on the bridge opened up at them.
Page and co-pilot Norman Elton watched the shells burst. At
about 2,000 ft, to their dismay, Carr's Horsa was blown to
pieces, part of its undercarriage striking them. 'We could see
men, still holding their weapons, falling in the air. Then the
port wing of the second glider was shot off, the aircraft
turned over and plunged to earth. I'd been diving already.
Now I dived like mad.'

Shell-bursts followed them. One, just under the glider,
seemed to Page to stop their descent. They raced down again.
The bridge-raiders had been equipped with arrester
parachutes for landing. Near the ground, Page released the
gear, felt the sudden drag, then was hurtling on. As the chute
opened, half the tail of the glider, to which it was fixed, had
come away with it, weakened by German fire. Suddenly they

had cleared a ,hedge, gone through four or five more and slewed to a lurching halt. Bullets were clipping the glider's roof.

'We'd landed about 600 yds from the bridge, near an unfinished portion of autobahn. It wasn't the planned position but at least we were down without much injury. One man had a broken arm. There were some German soldiers on the road and we exchanged shots, then headed for the river at top speed. I was running with Norman. One of the infantry lads fell. We pulled him up, but he was dead. Another was shot as we charged on.'

Reaching the water, the men from Page's glider made for the bridge under cover of the steep banks. Troops from other gliders were attacking on the far side, scrambling towards the dozen or so houses near the metal span. 'Shots were coming from windows. I sprayed one with my sten. Grenades were bursting. The glider troops went straight in. It was all over in ten minutes. The Germans in the house I entered gave themselves up. Our briefing had been right enough—there were about 200 of them around the bridge.'

Other Issel bridges were captured as rapidly, the glider men joined as they dug in by paratroops dropped outside their own zones. Page was startled at the northern bridge by soldiers who looked like 'extras' from a Western film—a unit of US parachute infantry who had jumped in Red Indian warpaint.

To their south, the Wacos came down in droves. The fortunes of their pilots closely mirrored those of the British crews. Major Nevins of Kansas City side-slipped into the landing zone in a Waco bearing his wife's name, Mary Lou. Missing a wrecked transport plane, Nevins yanked his wing up, lost a wheel in a ditch and spun to a standstill. As the stunned and airsick troops reeled out they were engaged by a dozen snipers in nearby buildings.

American pilot Wes Hare and his passengers were pinned down for more than two hours after landing. They were lucky to be alive. Hare's glider had dived straight in as he approached the ground, striking before he could correct its flight.

Flight Officer Vossler's trip had been uneventful until he released and heard bullets tearing through the glider's floor. Suddenly the Waco hesitated, trembled, then sped crazily towards a line of telephone poles. Next moment, Vossler had landed safely. Amazingly, the phone wires had arrested his mad plunge.

Heavy flak was pounding the combinations as Lieutenant Clarence J. Benkoski broke from his tow-ship. A glider ahead lost a wing and spiralled into the Diersfordter Wald. Benkoski's own tug was hit. Seconds later, a burst of fire entered the Waco behind the pilots, struck the jeep in the back and tore the glider's roof. It was pierced again as it descended, Benkoski encountering some of the few anti-glider posts in the area. Careering into them, the Waco skipped an irrigation ditch, smashed through a fence and stopped the other side. The jeep was unloaded. Despite the flak damage, it proved serviceable.

Gun fights were raging in most zones as American and British gliders dropped through the smoke, often landing in the same fields. Boucher-Giles had come down in a no-man's-land between the British airlanding sector and that of the US 17th Division. As German fire reduced his party, the survivors joined men from other gliders in a bid to clear the enemy. Doped with morphia, the wounded pilot was left near his Horsa in a shallow trench. As the day passed, he drifted between unconsciousness and semi-consciousness, alone save for corpses and the desultory attention of a German sniper whose bullets missed.

Eventually, hearing voices, Boucher-Giles cocked his pistol and raised a challenge. 'Hiya, Bud!' came the reply, and he found cigars and candy thrust in his hands. The Americans, a patrol of airborne troops, took him to their casualty station where a blood transfusion and more morphia were followed by mortar bombs and an attack by German infantry. Twice the post was evacuated under fire. Prudently, the Americans removed his ammunition after Boucher-Giles opened up from his stretcher with the pistol at surrounding trees.

Other glider men encountered the unexpected. A group of pilots, advancing by a farmhouse at the height of battle, saw German girls waving to them from windows as if they were friendly visitors. Dead cows were floating feet uppermost in the pond, an aerial dog-fight swirling high above. Miller was searching a barn when he found a Russian boy, perhaps 14 years old, hiding from him there. The lad had been brought from the eastern front. 'Once he saw I wouldn't harm him,' Miller recalls, 'I couldn't shake him off. He brought me water and apples, tried to give me a cigarette lighter, and insisted that I take him to England. I was far from convinced I'd be getting back.'

Sergeant-Pilot McEwan had done a good job. At the head of his glider troops the 'three weeks soldier' had advanced from the Hamilcar, eventually guarding some prisoners in a country house. Disconcertingly, the house was then attacked by the Americans. McEwan 'surrendered' to them.

By mid-day, Hamminkeln had been taken by the glider troops. The first to enter, after clearing the outskirts of skirmishes, were two platoons of the Devons accompanied by three glider pilots. Others joined them, their task to supervise prisoners and civilians while the Devons made headquarters in the schoolhouse. At a local hotel, the proprietor, Hans Neu, stoutly refused to serve glider pilots when they arrived. With the baker, he was ordered to produce food. Civilians were assembled in two churches and a large hall as the troops prepared to hold the town against counter-attack. Firing from both sides inflicted damage. One pilot watched the body of an old woman carried on boards amidst grieving relatives.

Meanwhile, the commander of the 6th Airborne Division, Major-General Eric Bols, had landed in a Horsa flown by Major Hugh Bartlett, a county cricketer. Finding the spot chosen for divisional headquarters untenable due to stiff opposition, Bols and Bartlett were scouting for a new location as HQ personnel from other gliders tried to reach the first venue. Bols was not alone in his problem. Ridgway himself, commanding the airborne army, confronted the fluidity of the battle at first hand, accounting (like Urquhart before him) for at least one of the enemy in skirmishes.

That afternoon, Bartlett met Toler, the Arnhem veteran, commanding a glider squadron assigned to the same landing zone. Both Bartlett's and Toler's squadrons had been assisted by the advent, unplanned, of American parachutists in their area, but many of their planes had been hit on landing. Bartlett reported that a number had been burnt out, most carrying petrol in jeeps or cans. Unlike his fellow officer, Toler had found his objective captured and had gone on to occupy the next farm. Leaving Bartlett, he decided to extend his position before nightfall.

Squadron Leader Huntley found his rendezvous, a dwelling west of Hamminkeln, on fire, and none of his pilots in the vicinity. The discovery completed a rude welcome. At 2,000 ft Huntley had been forced to take evasive action against concentrated flak; at rather more than 200 ft he had been hit and obliged to crash-land. On the ground, the glider was shot at and its jeep immobilised. The load was abandoned by the crew.

Everywhere, troops were piling from gliders and taking cover. In the fields behind the forest, they drew breath. Then, still dazed by the ride, they were embroiled in gun battles with German infantry. Men of the Ulster Rifles landed almost on top of two companies of Germans with armoured cars and half-tracks. Helped by the glider pilots and a band of Americans, they destroyed the heavy six-wheeled fighting vehicles and drove off the half-tracks. Within an hour the landing zone and its environs south of Hamminkeln were in Allied hands. From here the Ulsters seized a railway crossing and goods yard outside the town.

At the station, men from Reynolds's Horsa had cleared the flak battery. Every glider in the squadron had been hit, but

Reynolds, joined by his surviving pilots, attacked more gun pits in the neighbourhood. RAF glider pilots were prominent. One fired the PIAT which knocked out the first pit; another led a flanking attack on a second post. The German battery commander showed a white flag.

Though confused, the news which filtered through to Murray encouraged him. The Rhine bridgehead was growing, elements of the 15th Division fighting forward by the Diersfordter Wald. 'I felt confident,' recalls the colonel, 'that the Second Army would reach us the next day, and said as much to the glider pilots. They weren't convinced. They had heard that tale at Arnhem, they reminded me.'

As night came on the plain, the skymen crouched in freshly-dug trenches, waiting anxiously. German tanks were prowling beyond the Issel and, to the west, the snouts of heavy guns reared among black pines. Around them, the German forward divisions faced the Rhine, separating the air troops from Allied assault groups on the east bank. Nerves were taut. Miller, manning a Vickers-gun, heard shuffling to his front and, fingering the trigger, made out the shape of a steer in time to hold fire.

Reynolds's pilots ducked as 40 mm and Spandau missiles flew across the Issel from Tiger and Panther tanks. One bridge was blown by the glider troops for fear the tanks would force it and surge into Hamminkeln with German infantry. At Hans Neu's hostelry, pilots lay by loaded brens. Others guarded the civilians in darkened buildings. Shingleton, standing watch in a gloomy nave, provided syrup and water for grizzling tots.

At five minutes to midnight, American glider pilots dug in on the Wesel road were attacked by a tank, two gun-wagons and German troops. Flames lit the scene as tracer kindled a grounded glider and nearby house. While machine-guns and cannons thundered, pilot Jacob Zichterman plied his carbine. Repeatedly Zichterman aimed at Germans outlined in the glow, but none of them seemed to suffer. About the same time, Flight Officer Karl Harold was surprised in his trench by two Germans with rifles levelled. One asked how many men were with him. Hands raised, the glider pilot replied that his captors were outnumbered ten to one. They handed their guns to him.

Lieutenant St John anticipated no such luck. Experienced colleagues were already dead. Staff-Sergeant Harrison had died leaving his glider; Captain Norton's letters of the night before were the last he would ever write. Now, as St John clutched his rifle in the shadows, it appeared to him that half Hitler's army was moving through the dusky trees. He could hear voices, the muffled clatter of soldiers in such strength that resistance would be suicidal. 'There were just a few of us at a farm; we daren't challenge them.'

Lying low, St John waited in the lengthening night.

22

Receding Thunder

In straggling companies the men of the German 84th
Division drew abreast the farm, then continued east as the
pilots watched. With the marchers were gunners from the
massive pieces in the Diersfordter Wald. Clearly, they were not
deploying but withdrawing as the Second Army crossed the
Rhine in increasing strength. St John remembers the relief at
his own post. 'They could have wiped us out. Instead, they
ignored us, wanting only to escape while they had a chance.'

For the men of Arnhem, it was the reckoning—a
duplication of their retreat from Oosterbeek, the roles
reversed. In Toler's sector, a company of 74 Germans
surrendered when machine-gunned. Most were artillerymen
pulling back from the forest, or second-category infantry,
but a few were from parachute divisions. In the south,
capitulations to American skymen mounted rapidly. News of
developments filled the watchful air troops with buoyant
confidence.

As dawn touched the wood west of Bols's headquarters,
the crews of three light tanks landed by Hamilcars stretched
their limbs. A dozen glider pilots had acted as guards for
them through the night. Now they brewed tea and joked with
the men of the Devons who had shared their task. It was Palm
Sunday, 25 March. Major Peter Jackson, a glider pilot since

the inception of the regiment, prepared to celebrate with a quiet day 'drinking Schnapps and watching our Typhoons blast the enemy'.

Word of the night's events was soon passing by radio. The force beleaguered at Speldrop had been relieved and the British 152nd Brigade was advancing north of the Diersfordter Wald. The American Ninth Army had taken Dinslaken, its engineers the first to bridge the Rhine. Their 1,150-ft 'treadway' had been in use before dark. The Second Army had pontoons across the stream. Unlike the Holland operation, when tactical air support for the sky troops had faltered, the British Second Tactical Air Force and the US 29th Tactical Air Command had provided constant co-operation on this enterprise. Almost 8,000 attack-sorties had been flown the first day, at the cost of 56 planes.

This time, no mistakes had been made on the supply drop. Glider pilots had watched four-engined Liberators roar in at roof-top height, their baskets bouncing on target like rubber balls. 'They were so low,' reported one glider man, 'you could see the pilots waving as they charged past. The Germans couldn't believe their eyes. A prisoner who spoke English told me the flight was propaganda to boost our spirits. Some propaganda! It was a splendid sight.'

While quiet elation spread through the landing zones, German guns beyond the Issel answered sullenly. Shell and mortar fire landed on Hamminkeln. Four women were killed, and some wounded, when the church they occupied received a hit. Others were moved to a cellar beneath a brewery for greater safety. Reports of Schmeisser fire put glider pilots in the town on a new alert. Staff-Sergeant Brown was shaving when ordered, with others, to investigate. Grabbing a bren-gun, he accompanied Miller to the shelled church and clambered over the rubble to the tower above.

They scanned the landscape. Miller recollects an undisturbed scene. 'I couldn't see any sign of a fresh attack. If the Germans were there, they were well hidden. It was remarkably tranquil on our perch, apart from Nigel Brown's disgruntlement at having been disturbed in his toilet. It looked like a false alarm.'

Then the pilots heard the rumble of heavy tanks. 'My heart sank. All I could think of was Arnhem; of the night their armour crawled up to us. The light tanks from the gliders didn't growl like that. At last, they came in sight—the vehicles we had waited nine days to see at Oosterbeek—Monty's tanks. It was beautiful. Bar the cheering, the show was over when the Second Army came through.'

By the afternoon, advanced elements of the Second and Ninth Armies had reached the airborne forces at many points. In the British sector, the first to appear behind the Diersfordter Wald included the 6th Guards Armoured Brigade and men of the King's Own Scottish Borderers. Clusters of grinning sky troops applauded as the units passed. At field medical stations, injured glider pilots joined the cheering as news arrived that the line of evacuation was now clear.

None knew better than the medical staff of the division what the air troops had been through. Glider casualties, though fewer than some estimates, were severe, outnumbering those of the paratroops by three to one. Twenty-eight operations on critical cases were performed at just one field station, most involving multiple battle wounds.

Among the wounded were 77 glider pilots of the British force, another 175 of them killed or missing. Of these casualties (amounting to about 28 per cent of the pilots on the mission) rather more were sustained by RAF glider pilots than the army men. Something like 300 of their gliders had been hit by flak, and 32 had burnt out. Yet most had landed where planned, or not far away. Sydney St John's duties included helping an airborne padre to collect the bodies of dead comrades on a farm cart. The first he picked up had been shot dead on the exact spot he himself would have landed had the smoke not diverted him by about 300 yds.

Sorrow and triumph mingled. Every single objective had been accomplished with such speed that the survivors were often heady on their success. Glider pilots, searching the Diersfordter Wald for fugitives, heard shouting and laughter among the trees. Investigating, they discovered a party of paratroops, stripped to the waist save for their berets, treating an audience of prisoners to a rodeo show on German horses.

'For an hour or two,' asserts Shingleton, 'the ordeal had been worse than Arnhem, but we got the hell over first; after that, there was no stopping us.' Indeed, the landing was a stunning stroke, the *magnum opus* of the glider war—ingenious, finely organised, daringly executed at high risk. To what extent the unexpected smoke bore on losses is debatable. In Murray's opinion it was 'incredible' that casualties were not greater in view of the impediment. On the other hand, a clearer sky might actually have increased the accuracy of anti-aircraft fire.

According to one summary of the British mission, 60 per cent of the glider effort 'came off'—more than enough, as events proved. Of the overall air assault, Ridgway wrote:

> The airborne drop in depth destroyed enemy gun and rear defensive positions in one day—positions it might have taken many days to reduce by ground attack. The impact of the airborne divisions at one blow shattered hostile defence and permitted the prompt link-up with ground troops. The increased bridgehead materially assisted the build-up essential for subsequent success. The insistent drive to the east and rapid seizure of key terrain were decisive to subsequent developments, permitting Allied armour to debouch into the North German plain at full strength and momentum.

As the Germans retreated, the sky army netted prisoners in large numbers. Ridgway watched 2,500 of them being escorted to the Rhine by American glider pilots. Sniping and shellfire were still a threat, German aircraft occasionally cutting in to straffe and bomb. Winston Churchill, anxious to inspect the Wesel bridgehead, was turned back by the

American commander in the area. Lieutenant-General William H. Simpson refused to accept responsibility for the safety of the prime minister. Soon, Murray's men were withdrawing by squadrons across the broad stream.

Already, on the west bank, supply units had provided showers and kitchens where the fliers could wash and feed as they moved back. One camp, dubbed The Rhine Hotel, displayed a sign proclaiming 'Glider Pilots a Speciality'. Here, for a few hours, they rested, listening to the receding thunder of a dying war. Within a fortnight, railway trains would be crossing a new bridge at Wesel, built by US sappers; the Ruhr surrounded by Allied forces. A week after leaving England, the Britons who had steered their gliders to Germany were flying home.

On arrival at the airfield, Down Ampney, they were confronted by the customs service with entry papers. 'I was asked,' recalls one pilot, 'what I had to declare from my trip abroad.' He was not amused. Reported Murray forbearingly: 'Some delay was caused by each glider pilot having to complete forms. Luckily, after 300 had done so, they [the customs officials] ran out of forms.'

With the war in its last weeks, two projects tantalised the air army planners under Eisenhower. One was for a scheme to land gliders and parachute forces near Kassel, Germany, in the greatest airborne offensive yet organised.

Four American and two British sky divisions would be used, it was proposed, to seize airfields and strips in the area, after which infantry would be flown in by transport planes. When a sufficient force was in the airhead—nine divisions were visualised—it would be deployed against enemy communications ahead of Allied armies striking behind the Ruhr.

The other plan, code-named 'Eclipse', envisaged the capture of Berlin from its ultimate guard of diehard Nazis by parachutists and glider troops. As a preliminary, fleets of Horsas, Wacos and transports would stream to Templehof

Airport and the Luftwaffe fields round the capital. From here, the attack would be pressed to the rubble-strewn boulevards, the parks, the Reich Chancellery. Mooted as far back as autumn 1944, the scheme might indeed have eclipsed not only the last days of the Führer but also Russian plans to take Berlin.

The ideas came to nothing. So rapid was the Allied advance that the Kassel project became pointless, while 'Eclipse' was overtaken by Yalta and a deal between the big powers. Wesel was to be the last outing of the glider fleets.

Few regrets were expressed by the glider troops. There had been little to envy in their frightening role as passengers, often to novice pilots, in flimsy, uncomfortable and defenceless craft, liable to force-land any time after taking off. If their tug-planes did not fail, if their towlines did not break, if they were not peppered by shrapnel or bullets as they travelled, they could look forward to terminating their journey with a juddering crash and a welcome of gunfire or mortar bombs.

Less than half the 6th Airborne Division was alive and unscathed at the war's end (the US 17th Airborne Division had sustained 1,346 casualties on the Rhine). At least the paratroops were distinguished by a glamorous public image. By contrast, the glider soldier was regarded widely as just another infantryman. He got a lift; he did not get a parachute. Generals sympathised. Not many high rankers went for glider trips.

In the East, some small operations saw the struggle out. American gliders landed engineering equipment during the final stages of the Burma campaign, and a few Wacos were used on Luzon, in the Pacific, to make contact with Philippine guerrillas there. But interest lapsed and the Allied nations soon neglected their glider fleets. Though Britain's Glider Pilot Regiment was maintained until 1957, its campaigns after the Rhine—in Palestine, Korea, Malaya and elsewhere—were not in gliders and its numbers were much reduced.

The 1950s were rich in new developments. Faster and more versatile transport planes; parachute techniques for dropping tanks and guns; above all, helicopters replaced the wooden chariots. The glider pilots look back now with mixed thoughts. 'We volunteered and took the rough with the smooth,' says Bob Cardy. 'We made friends; we lost some.' Of 3,302 officers and other ranks who took part in the operations of the Glider pilot Regiment, 551 were killed and 750 either wounded or taken prisoner. A total of 172 received awards for gallantry and distinguished service.

Their gliders, left on disused airfields or where they fell in action, eventually rotted or were vandalized. Many pilots have since returned, some repeatedly, to the woods and meadows where they lurched down. From time to time reminders of the past emerge. 'The trees are thinner,' reflects Des Page, who regularly visits Oosterbeek; 'there's been a lot of elm disease. They have to fell them the old way. The chain-saws broke. They kept grinding on the shrapnel that's in the trunks.'

Recommended Reading

Few books have been published on war gliders. Readers interested in pursuing the subject may be helped by a short note of some the author has found useful and enjoyable.

The first account of the exploits of the Glider Pilot Regiment was Ronald Seth's *Lion With Blue Wings* (Gollancz, 1955). Most later writers owe a debt to this foundation work, which has forewords by Viscount Alanbrooke and Air-Chief-Marshal Sir Leslie Hollinghurst. Readers with regimental connections may like to know that it contains a roll of honour for the period 1942–5.

In 1962 Brigadier George Chatterton published his own story of the regiment, *The Wings of Pegasus* (Macdonald). Including a preliminary chapter on his RAF and army career prior to joining the glider force, the book is valuable as a first-hand account of the development and deployment of the Glider Pilot Regiment by the man who was not only its commander but, as Colonel Murray recalls, 'very much its inspiration and driving force'. Brigadier Chatterton's book is dedicated to young people, many of whom have his efforts and resourcefulness to thank for the glider flying they have enjoyed with the regimental association at Haddenham.

Lawrence Wright's *The Wooden Sword* (Elek, 1967) follows

British glider operations from the viewpoint of a pre-war sailplane enthusiast who became closely involved with planning on the RAF side. The author's urbane recollections take in the earliest pioneering days of the glider unit, the 'back room' aspect of operations and pertinent statistics for the main missions.

The Red Devils by Major G. G. Norton (Leo Cooper, 1971) tells the story of the British airborne forces as a whole, devoting (since it takes events up to 1967) rather more space to paratroops than gliders. Nevertheless, as a summary of operations, backed by good maps and photographs, it is lucid. The book includes a chronology of British airborne history and a note on the airborne forces museum at Aldershot, which was founded by Major Norton.

The most exhaustive work on military gliders rests to the credit of Colonel James E. Mrazek, himself a World War II glider man, whose *The Glider War* (Robert Hale and St Martin's Press, 1975) is a first-rate account of American, German, British and other glider operations. Colonel Mrazek is good to read, his information wide-ranging, and the pictures and campaign maps are excellent. From the same author and publishers, *Fighting Gliders of World War II* (1977) provides a useful companion book, including 162 illustrations of military gliders with notes on their development and technical data.

Milton Dank, another wartime glider pilot, draws on his experiences in the American service to give *The Glider Gang* (Lippincott, 1977) its punchy authenticity. Without aiming for Mrazek's range, the author makes good use of glider pilot reminiscence to take a fast-moving trip through the major operations.

General Bibliography

Bauer, Cornelius, *The Battle of Arnhem*. London, Hodder & Stoughton, 1966

Bredin, Lt-Col A. E. C., *Three Assault Landings*, London, Gale & Polden, 1946

Chatterton, Brigadier George, *The Wings of Pegasus*, London, Macdonald, 1962

Churchill, Winston S., *The Second World War* (vols 1–6), London, Cassell, 1955

Cole, Lt-Col Howard, *On Wings of Healing*, London, Blackwood, 1963

Deane-Drummond, Anthony, *Return Ticket*, London, Collins, 1953

Eisenhower, Dwight D., *Crusade in Europe*, London, Heinemann, 1948

Ellis, Major L. F. *Victory in the West*, London, HMSO, 1968

Gale, Lt-Gen Sir Richard, *With the 6th Airborne Division in Normandy*, London, Sampson Low Marston, 1948

Gavin, Lt-Gen James M., *War and Peace in the Space Age*, London, Hutchinson, 1959

Glider Pilot Regimental Association, *The Eagle* (vol 2), London, 1945

Hagen, Louis, *Arnhem Lift*, London, Pilot Press, 1945

Heydte, Baron von der, *Daedelus Returned: Crete 1941*, London, Hutchinson, 1958

Horrocks, Lt-Gen Sir Brian, *A Full Life*, London, Leo Cooper, 1974

Ismay, General Lord, *Memoirs*, London, Heinemann, 1960

Kronfeld, Robert, *Kronfeld on Gliding and Soaring*, London, John Hamilton, 1932

Lockhart, Robert Bruce, *Comes the Reckoning*, London, Putnam, 1950

Mason, Herbert Malloy, *The Rise of the Luftwaffe 1918–1940*, London, Cassell, 1975

Ministry of Information, *By Air to Battle*, London, HMSO, 1945

Monks, Noel, *Eye Witness*, London, Muller, 1955

Moorehead, Alan, *Eclipse*, London, Hamish Hamilton, 1945

Morgan, Lt-General Sir Frederick, *Overture to Overlord*, London, Hodder & Stoughton, 1950

Mrazek, James E., *The Glider War*, London, Robert Hale, 1975

Mrazek, James E., *Fighting Gliders of World War II*, London, Robert Hale, 1977

North, John, *North-West Europe 1944–5: the Achievements of the 21st Army Group*, London, HMSO, 1943

Norton, G. G., *The Red Devils: the Story of the British Airborne Forces*, London, Leo Cooper, 1971

Otway, Colonel Terence, *The Second World War 1939–45: Airborne Forces*, London, War Office, 1946

Packe, M., *First Airborne*, London, Secker & Warburg, 1948

Poston, Hay & Scott, *Design and Development of Weapons*, London, HMSO, 1964

Ridgway, Matthew B., *Soldier: the Memoirs of Matthew B. Ridgway*, New York, Harper, 1956

Ryan, Cornelius, *The Longest Day*, London, Gollancz, 1960

Ryan, Cornelius, *A Bridge Too Far*, London Hamish Hamilton, 1974

Saunders, Hilary St George, *The Red Beret*, London, Michael Joseph, 1950

Seth, Ronald, *Lion With Blue Wings*, London, Gollancz, 1955

Shulman, Milton, *Defeat in the West*, London, Secker & Warburg, 1947

Sosabowski, Maj-Gen Stanislaw, *Freely I Served*, London, William Kimber, 1960

Urquhart, Maj-Gen R. E., *Arnhem*, London, Cassell, 1958

Weller, George, *The Story of the Paratroops*, New York, Random House, 1958

Wright, Lawrence, *The Wooden Sword*, London, Elek, 1967

Index

Bestselling Fiction

☐ Saudi	Laurie Devine	£2.95
☐ Lisa Logan	Marie Joseph	£2.50
☐ The Stationmaster's Daughter	Pamela Oldfield	£2.95
☐ Duncton Wood	William Horwood	£3.50
☐ Aztec	Gary Jennings	£3.95
☐ The Pride	Judith Saxton	£2.99
☐ Fire in Heaven	Malcolm Bosse	£3.50
☐ Communion	Whitley Strieber	£3.50
☐ The Ladies of Missalonghi	Colleen McCullough	£2.50
☐ Skydancer	Geoffrey Archer	£2.50
☐ The Sisters	Pat Booth	£3.50
☐ No Enemy But Time	Evelyn Anthony	£2.95

Prices and other details are liable to change

ARROW BOOKS, BOOKSERVICE BY POST, PO BOX 29, DOUGLAS, ISLE OF MAN, BRITISH ISLES

NAME...

ADDRESS..

....

....

Please enclose a cheque or postal order made out to Arrow Books Ltd. for the amount due and allow the following for postage and packing.

U.K. CUSTOMERS: Please allow 22p per book to a maximum of £3.00.

B.F.P.O. & EIRE: Please allow 22p per book to a maximum of £3.00

OVERSEAS CUSTOMERS: Please allow 22p per book.

Whilst every effort is made to keep prices low it is sometimes necessary to increase cover prices at short notice. Arrow Books reserve the right to show new retail prices on covers which may differ from those previously advertised in the text or elsewhere.

Bestselling Fiction

☐ Hiroshmia Joe	Martin Booth	£2.95
☐ The Pianoplayers	Anthony Burgess	£2.50
☐ Queen's Play	Dorothy Dunnett	£3.95
☐ Colours Aloft	Alexander Kent	£2.95
☐ Contact	Carl Sagan	£3.50
☐ Talking to Strange Men	Ruth Rendell	£5.95
☐ Heartstones	Ruth Rendell	£2.50
☐ The Ladies of Missalonghi	Colleen McCullough	£2.50
☐ No Enemy But Time	Evelyn Anthony	£2.95
☐ The Heart of the Country	Fay Weldon	£2.50
☐ The Stationmaster's Daughter	Pamela Oldfield	£2.95
☐ Erin's Child	Sheelagh Kelly	£3.99
☐ The Lilac Bus	Maeve Binchy	£2.50

Prices and other details are liable to change

ARROW BOOKS, BOOKSERVICE BY POST, PO BOX 29, DOUGLAS, ISLE OF MAN, BRITISH ISLES

NAME...

ADDRESS...

....

....

Please enclose a cheque or postal order made out to Arrow Books Ltd. for the amount due and allow the following for postage and packing.

U.K. CUSTOMERS: Please allow 22p per book to a maximum of £3.00.

B.F.P.O. & EIRE: Please allow 22p per book to a maximum of £3.00

OVERSEAS CUSTOMERS: Please allow 22p per book.

Whilst every effort is made to keep prices low it is sometimes necessary to increase cover prices at short notice. Arrow Books reserve the right to show new retail prices on covers which may differ from those previously advertised in the text or elsewhere.